Looking Into Intranets and the Internet

Advice for Managers

Anita Rosen

amacom

American Management Association

New York • Atlanta • Boston • Chicago • Kansas City • San Francisco • Washington, D.C.
Brussels • Mexico City • Tokyo • Toronto

This publication is designed to provide accurate and authoritative
information in regard to the subject matter covered. It is sold with the
understanding that the publisher is not engaged in rendering legal,
accounting, or other professional service. If legal advice or other expert
assistance is required, the services of a competent professional person
should be sought.

Library of Congress Cataloging-in-Publication Data

Rosen, Anita.
    Looking into intranets and the Internet : advice for managers /
Anita Rosen.
        p.   cm.
    Includes index.
    ISBN 0-8144-7948-0
    1. Business enterprises—Computer networks.   2. Intranets
(Computer networks)—Case studies.   3. Internet marketing—Case
studies.   4. Internet advertising—Case studies.   I. Title.
HD30.37.R67   1997
650'.0285'46—dc21   96-39952
                                                            CIP

Printing number

10   9   8   7   6   5   4   3   2   1

Contents

Preface

The goal of this book is to help you make clear, intelligent decisions on how and where to implement Internet technologies in your company or organization. It resolves the following issues that businesspeople want to know about Internet technology:

- Technology
  - —Understanding the terminology and technology behind the Internet
  - —Understanding how to integrate Internet technology into your company's direction
  - —Having enough comprehension of the technology to work with technologists
  - —Understanding the cost of the technology
- Business applications
  - —Figuring out if your business will benefit from Internet technology
  - —Understanding how using Internet technology can meet your company's objectives
  - —Creating an effective Internet business case to solve your business applications
  - —Understanding the cost of creating and supporting a site
  - —Properly focusing the information in your site to meet your goals
- Internet content
  - —Deciding on Internet applications
  - —Evaluating intranet applications

—Using the Internet to provide information to customers without providing too much information to competitors
—Guidelines for creating Internet sites that will meet your needs
—Providing an effective repository of information for employees

- Focusing your site
—Getting started
—Defining your company's Internet direction
—Creating a site that meets the stated direction
—Establishing site goals and building sites that meet those goals
—Maximizing the effectiveness of an existing Internet site
—Communicating your ideas effectively using Internet technology
—Supporting remote locations using the Internet
—Managing and controlling Internet/intranet content
—Keeping your site focused to obtain maximum results

- Managing your site
—Managing requests that come via the Internet
—Identifying components that make a good Internet site
—Protecting your company and your site from intruders
—Deciding on and managing external resources employees may have access to
—Staffing a site and providing timely feedback to inquiries

- Staffing considerations
—Identifying what kinds of people you will need to create, support, and manage your site
—Managing Internet technology contractors
—Deciding what percentage of your web site should be built internally and what percentage should be built by contractors
—Identifying the number of people you will need and the skill sets they will need to possess to manage or support a web site, and calculating the cost of hiring these employees
—Identifying existing employees who could migrate to Internet-related jobs

—Planning and managing new business traffic generated by an Internet site
- Solving employee problems before they happen
  —Setting intranet guidelines before problems erupt
  —Setting guidelines for Internet web sites
  —Setting guidelines for intranet web pages
  —Setting guidelines for e-mail
- Marketing your site
  —Creating an effective web site launch
  —Using an Internet web site as an integrated component of your company's marketing and sales programs
  —Getting employees and customers to feel comfortable using intranet applications

I was inspired to write this book by friends' and clients' myriad inquiries regarding the benefits and practicality of creating a web site for their company or organization. I have spent the past sixteen years working in the computer industry creating business and market plans, and project managing new technologies. I work as a "hired gun" for companies that need someone to come in and get difficult products released or to help them plan or implement market strategies. Most recently I have worked for Netscape and Oracle. At Netscape I implemented the SuiteSpot family of product's 2.0 release. When I told people I was at Netscape, I usually was asked one of two questions: First, how was Netscape going to make money? Second, how would a web site benefit their company? Since the Internet technology is so new, and questions were constant, I figured that many people I didn't know had the same questions. When I went to the local bookstores I found a profusion of Internet technology books but no Internet business books. So I wrote this book to answer the questions that businesspeople would have regarding the Internet.

I am interested in your feedback. I would like to know if this book helps you to implement an Internet/intranet. You can reach me at acrosen@best.com;www.best.com/~acrosen/ or run a search on Anita Rosen Consulting using an Internet search engine.

A.R.

1

Internet/Intranet Overview

Everywhere you turn these days it seems like you are hearing something about the Internet. Either it's a story about an Internet company or it's a company advertising their WWW (World Wide Web) location. The question that many people in companies and organizations are asking themselves is, Do I need to be on the Internet?

The goal of this book is to take the reader through the decision-making process of figuring out if an Internet site is right for your company or organization. Once you figure out if your company can benefit from an Internet site, you are taken through the logical progression of deciding how to create and present a successful Internet business case. After showing how to build your business case the book takes you through the process of creating and marketing an effective Internet site.

This book is broken down into seven chapters. Chapter 1 is designed to be an overview of the Internet industry. Specifically this chapter answers the questions why now, and why the Internet? This chapter also reviews some of the most common concerns companies have about using Internet technology. Chapter 2 is designed to be a minitechnology primer. The goal of Chapter 2 is to give you enough background on the technology so that you can feel comfortable with the Internet, understand articles written about the Internet, and make informed Internet decisions. Chapter 3 takes you through the process of identifying how your organization can best use Internet technology. Chapter 4 presents six business cases and shows you how to effectively create your own business case. Chapter 5 explains how to manage the design of an Internet, and Chapter 6 explains how to manage the development of an Internet. Finally you are taken through an Internet launch process and are shown how best to market your site.

Why Is There All This Hype With Internet Companies?

The most visible company when it comes to the Internet is Netscape. There was a good reason the financial community had such an overwhelming response to Netscape when the company went public. Netscape provided the information industry with a paradigm shift. Their business plan was evolutionary and logical since it utilized known technologies in a new and enlightened manner. The Internet has been around for years, providing a proven infrastructure for interorganizational communications. Netscape's founders saw the existing Internet as a technology that could be utilized on a greater scale by businesses and organizations. They saw that there were four facilitating technologies that had reached a level of critical mass that would allow the Internet technology to be easily utilized by nontechnology people. The infrastructure technologies that facilitated the explosion of the Internet are (1) Transmission Control Protocol/Internet Protocol (TCP/IP), the universal internetworking protocol, (2) low-cost, high-speed modems, (3) proliferation of PCs, and (4) graphical user interfaces (GUIs). These technologies will be explained in depth in Chapter 2.

How Does the Internet Philosophy Differ From Conventional Technology Direction?

Companies demanded and the computer industry recognized the need businesses and organizations had for instantaneous information to be accessed within a company and between companies. Until 1995 the client-server technology model was the philosophy of choice for companies to support their growing, disparate computer environment. The client-server generation of technologies all touted intracompany collaborative capabilities, including e-mail and news groups. What the Internet provided was the next logical step in client-server technology. The Internet provides a simple, easy-to-use infrastructure that works on any computer, of any size, located anywhere. The Internet's open flow of information frees companies from trying to get different computers to work with one another. Companies can use the Internet as the basis of computer communications with other organizations. Before the Internet it was difficult or expensive to synchronize different groups' computers so they could work with each other. Internet technology makes communications and access transparent, so that anyone can work with anyone else regardless of the type of computer used.

What Is the Current Direction for Organizations' Information Systems?

Increasing information flow increases employee efficiency. When employees have access to information at their desk, wherever their desk may be, less time is spent finding and re-creating information, and more time is spent intelligently processing and using information.

Outside of the enterprise companies are finding that to remain competitive they need to disseminate information faster and more easily to both vendors and customers. Businesses are finding that they need immediate, interactive capabilities that faxes and conference calls can't provide. Organizations that are attempting to maintain quality services on smaller budgets need more efficient mechanisms to support clients. For example, a salesperson on the road often ends up playing telephone tag with a customer. Voice mail helps, since detailed messages can be left. What if the customer asks for specific changes to a price list? The salesperson can send a fax and hope it is delivered and readable. With e-mail the information can be sent in its original spreadsheet form, making it easy to read, printable, and saving the customer the time of retyping the information. An additional benefit is that the salesperson has an audit trail of every e-mail sent and received in case questions arise later. If the company has an Internet site, popular information can reside on this site. Customers can independently access this site, increasing productivity and providing better support for customers. When customers have access to the latest information, they won't need to track down salespeople to get basic details.

How Will the Internet Impact My Organization?

The Internet is not an invasive technology. Companies do not need to change their existing way of doing business. The Internet runs on top of existing computer technologies. The only requirements for getting on the Internet are a computer, a modem (a device that lets a computer talk over phone lines), and access to the Internet (people can sign up with companies that provide Internet access; the most popular is America Online). The program that connects the person to the Internet is called a *web browser*. A web browser is a software program that lets a person on a computer view Internet web sites. The two most popular web browsers are The Navigator from Netscape and Internet Explorer from Microsoft. Since a good web browser is an intuitive tool, people can easily use their computer to access other computers and "surf the web." Organizations can use web browsers as windows to internal company web sites and create new business applications. Web sites that are internal to a company are called *intranets*. Using an intranet, individual departments can create web sites to inform or educate fellow employees about their department. Departments can create applications to support employees' work flow. For instance, finance can have the latest expense reports or time cards available on their site, while human resources might have job postings or benefits information posted on their site. Marketing can post the latest product information, while manufacturing can post the shipping schedules. Employees needing to find information do not need to call all over the company in their attempt to track down the latest schedule. Employees on an intranet can *bookmark* important sites and return to those sites on demand. Employees can be assured that the information they retrieve from a site will be the most recent information. An Internet web site can be created to provide customers with the latest information on your business. Web sites can provide potential customers with on-demand product, support, and ordering information.

Besides the inherent benefits of using Internet technology, companies are finding that Internet technology is low-cost and provides the latest functionality. When a company decides it wants to increase support to employees by providing outside access to the Internet, employees do not modify the way they are currently working. Employees who attempt to access outside information in a closed environment will receive a message that the outside site is not available. Once an employee has outside access the message is no longer displayed and the employee can access the site. This also applies to e-mail. An employee in a closed environment attempting to send e-mail to someone outside of the environment will receive a message that the system cannot access that e-mail address. If the company allows this person e-mail access outside of the organization, automatically the employee will be able to send and receive e-mail to people outside the organization. For example, a company currently has e-mail for employees to intracommunicate. Sales has been requesting access to their customers; purchasing wants access to their sources; marketing wants access to facilitate a partnership. No changes need to be made to the way people currently work. The company's computer support organization can easily provide a mail server to support intercompany communication.

Common Concerns

Some people have watched skeptically as Internet use has skyrocketed. They are concerned about the effect of the Internet on their company's infrastructure, security risks, and managing employees who have access to the Internet. The most common concerns that people have are answered below:

How can I integrate this new philosophy with my company's current infrastructure? Internet technology has coexisted with corporate technologies for years. Employees can run web browsers at their desk on their PC the same way they currently run other applications. Employees do not need to change the way they currently work. By using a web browser as an interface to business applications, companies can build an *intranet* (internal network) at their own speed. In the future companies can build applications using *plug-ins*. Plug-ins are programs that show up as an icon in the browser. When clicked, the plug-in activates a program or special utilities. For instance, a company can use a plug-in to access their stock inventory. When a customer calls to see if a product is in stock, the employee answering the phone clicks on the inventory icon in the browser, a page opens up on-screen, and the employee enters the name of the product in the space on the page. The plug-in application finds the information in the inventory database and provides the employee with the information.

There are distinct benefits to using Internet technology over existing technology to build these types of applications: the web browser's consistent user interface, the ease of building applications that run on many kinds of computers, the low price of Internet technologies, and the availability of the latest technologies. These applications can be augmented by providing pictures of the product. A small video or moving illustration can be created to explain how this product should be used. In the future the company may decide that they want customers to have direct access to the inventory program. Since the application was built using Internet technology, opening technology to external sources is straightforward. The company can decide how much access people outside of the company can have to the inventory application. Distributors might have access to the product's availability, distributor price list, and special promotions, while direct users might have access to installation instructions, availability, and list prices.

An easy way to get started with the new philosophy of the Internet within your company or organization is to use the web browser to introduce e-mail to employees. For employees new to e-mail there are many good e-mail interface applications out there. For example, Netscape's Navigator mail interface is simple and easy to use. Employees can start their day by clicking on the Navigator icon. The company can display the latest corporate news or company direction on the company's *home page* (opening screen). As departments start seeing the advantage to adding their information to the home page, employees gradually become comfortable with this new technology. When the envelope icon on the lower right-hand corner is clicked, all new e-mail messages are displayed.

Web applications can provide companies with simple, innovative new ways to support customers and extend market share. For instance, a market research company wants to support smaller clients. Traditionally clients had to purchase dedicated computer systems and dedicated lines (computer systems and phone lines that work only with this one special application) to access a proprietary system. Now, using a web browser, the company can create a plug-in for their application. This solution can be made available for all clients who use a standard *Internet service provider* (ISP) and use a web browser. By clicking on the company's icon, clients can run analysis applications on their computer, accessing the company's database through a password-protected interface. This solution is easy and inexpensive for both the company and the clients, allowing the company to provide better services, and access smaller markets, with relatively little cost to infrastructure and training.

What is the potential downside of using Internet/intranet technology? Many companies fear new technologies. They have experienced the "bleeding edge" (when technology is very new and does not work as easily as promised) and are afraid the technology cannot support their corporation. The brilliance of the Internet/intranet business model is that it uses known, proven technology currently in use in millions of sites today.

How can I keep my company's data secure? Businesspeople are besieged with news reports of computer security breaches. Securing company information is a high priority for any businessperson. It is reasonable to be concerned that new network technology may open a business up to security breaches. Any time a company allows nondedicated access (phone line access) to their information network, there is the chance of security breaches. A company is as safe as the precautions developed to deter intruders. There are many sophisticated security applications available for Internet technology. These security products are designed to protect companies and their data. Every company employing Internet/intranet technology should integrate a good security plan. Typically companies keep Internet applications separate from intranet applications. This is done by providing a separate computer for outside applications from that used for inside applications.

How can I keep my employees from spending their day surfing the Internet? If you manage your own site or hire an ISP to manage your site, there are utilities available that allow the *web master* (person who manages the web site) to grant employees complete, partial, or no access to the WWW. Access permissions can be as specific as an individual or as general as a department.

Now that you have an idea of what the Internet is, let's move to Chapter 2 and learn more about the technologies that support the Internet.

2

Technology Primer

This chapter is a minitechnology primer, designed to help you better understand the technology behind the Internet.

The Internet

The Internet is a collection of computers located all over the world that anyone can access. Graphical user interfaces (GUIs) called web browsers allow people to access these computers without having to learn cryptic computer commands. The growth of web browsers has dramatically altered the Internet. Traditionally technologists and scientists used the Internet to communicate with each other. Now, because of web browsers, companies and individuals can create interesting web pages with nice graphics. People with web access can "surf" web sites to learn more about companies and organizations, play games, or check out a friend's home page.

An Internet is open to the world, intranets are a closed network, and extranets are a hybrid. Internets, intranets, and extranets use the same technology. The difference is that intranets only let people within an organization access their computers. Intranets do not publish their location. Extranets let a selected group of people outside the company access the network. An example of an Internet is a company's World Wide Web site. An extranet is a site where, for example, customers may access pricing information by typing in their customer number and password. An intranet is accessible only within a company. The HR department might have an intranet site that explains 401(k) options.

Network Infrastructure

In the 1960s, users were connected directly to host computers. The users were referred to as *dumb users* or *dumb terminals* because no processing took place at the desktop. The central computer polled the end user to see if information was to be sent or received. When computer use began to grow, the need for computers to talk to one another created computer communications. At first information was sent asynchronously (one character at a time, with variable time intervals between characters) from one computer to another. In order for the receiving computer to know what was being sent, and the sending computer to know the format in which to send the information, communications designers created *protocols*. The first protocols were very simple. In order to better control information, it became necessary to define in detail how to send and receive information. This detail is described in *protocol stacks*. By the late sixties and early seventies, detailed protocol stacks had been developed.

Many companies have developed protocol stacks to explain and define how information is sent and received in their networks. The International Standards Organization (ISO), Digital Equipment Corporation (DEC), and IBM have defined similar seven-layer, fixed-format stacks. These stacks clearly explain and define the process necessary to send and receive information. None of these stacks have been embraced as stacks that future applications will be developed using since their structures tend to be hierarchical and fixed. A fixed hierarchical stack does not easily lend itself to the fast, effective networks needed today. Today's networks need to have the ability to skip layers in order to send information faster. Xerox's XNS stack is the model for "future stacks" because it was developed with exits. Exits provide the flexibility to allow layers to be skipped.

The ISO stack is a good example of all the levels of information needed in order to send and receive information. Each layer

Figure 2-1. Protocol Stack

	ISO		IBM SNA		DECnet	XNS (Xerox)	Novell	Apple	TCP/IP
7	Application	7	Transaction Services	7	Network Management	4 Application			
6	Presentation	6	Presentation Services	6	Network Application		Application	Application	Application
5	Session	5	Data Flow Control	5	Session Control	3 Control			
								Zone Information	
4	Transport	4	Transmission Control	4	End-to-End Commnctns	2 Transport Interprocess	IPX (Internet packet exchange)	Routing table Name binding	TCP Transport
3	Network	3	Path Control	3	Routing	1 Transport Internet		Datagram Delivery	IP Internet-working
2	Data Link	2	Data Link Control	2	Data Link	Ethernet X.25 Leased lines Other	Ethernet FDDI Token Ring Other	Ethernet FDDI talk Token talk Other	Network Interface
1	Physical	1	Physical Control	1	Physical				

in the seven-layer ISO stack defines the functions necessary to send or receive information from one computer to another.

Layer 0—Physical Media. Not usually mentioned in protocol stacks are the actual wires (media) being used. To send information from one computer to another, one of the following media is used: twisted pair wire (telephone wire or highgrade telephone wire called *shielded twisted pair*, DDS, ISDN, T1); fiber optics (long strands of glass, SONNET); coax cable (commonly used for cable TV, T3); or radio (satellite, or infrared—the same technology used for TV remote controls).

Layer 1—Physical internetworking devices. The devices send a series of 1s and 0s as bit streams over the wires. The physical layer describes activation, deactivation, and maintenance of the circuits that use the physical media as well as the mechanical and electrical specifications for the interfaces. Components like RS–232 connectors, multiplexers, repeaters, hubs, modems, data terminal equipment, and data communications equipment are all devices defined in layer 1.

Layer 2—Data link. The data link layer controls data flow, handles transmission errors, provides physical addressing, and manages access to physical media. This is where local area net-

Figure 2-2. ISO Protocol Stack

ISO

7	Application
6	Presentation
5	Session
4	Transport
3	Network
2	Data Link
1	Physical

works (LANs)—like a bus, star, or ring—along with bridges and switches are defined. Within a LAN, the protocols that ensure correct sharing of the physical media are defined in layer 2.

Layer 3—Network. The network layer provides path determination, path switching, and route processing functions. The intelligence within networks, such as network addresses, is located in layer 3. Common networks are IP (Internet Protocol), IPX (Novell), and DECnet (DEC). Hardware devices such as routers are defined and operate at the network level.

Layer 4—Transport. The purpose of the transport layer is to hide the different characteristics of the varying networks and to shield network performance from the users. Technologies found in layer 4 are TCP, UDP, or LU6.2 (IBM).

Layer 5—Session. The session layer manages and controls the dialogues between the users' applications. This is where one application talks with another application. Layer 5 defines how a customer database can be shared between multiple users or applications.

Layer 6—Presentation. The presentation layer is concerned with the syntax and context of the application protocols. The web browser is defined in this layer.

Layer 7—Application. Application defines how common services are provided. Applications defined in the application level are mail store and forward (X.400); virtual terminal; file transfer; remote database access; network management (SNMP) and remote procedure calls (RPCs), which allow interactive exchanges between applications.

Wide and Local Area Networks

In local area communications one computer is directly connected to another computer. The medium is owned by the network users. This is a LAN. Wide area communications is when a computer is connected through a communications service provider. The medium is owned by a network provider. Wide area networks (WANs) are provided by telephone companies, by cable companies, or through private satellite companies. Both

LANs and WANs use the same physical connections: twisted pair, fiber, coax, and radio.

LAN Speeds

Local area networks allow computers to communicate with each other. When buildings are built, computer-grade wires should be installed along with the phone wiring. Many companies use twisted pair to connect workstations to the wiring closet, and fiber to connect wiring closets to each other. Twisted pair comes in two different types: unshielded twisted pair (UTP) and shielded twisted pair (STP). Shielded twisted pair was developed by IBM. All STP is equivalent to the quality of category 5 UTP. There are five different types of STP. The different STP types denote what additional wires are found within the cable. UTP has varying degrees of quality and wires.

Table 2-1. LAN Speeds

Name	Speed
UTP Category 1, twisted pair	Poor quality (not found)
UTP Category 2, twisted pair	Voice grade
UTP Category 3 (10BaseT, T4) 4-pair twisted pair	Up to 100Mb
UTP Category 4 (IBM token ring) twisted pair	Up to 100Mb (better quality)
UTP Category 5, tx, 2-pair twisted pair	Up to 100Mb (best quality)
Thin coax (10Base2)	Up to 1 gigahertz
Thick coax (10Base5) (supports farther distances)	Up to 1 gigahertz
Fiber multimode (fx) 2-strand	1 gigahertz
Fiber single mode	10 gigahertz

WAN Speeds

WAN service providers have different names for each speed that is purchased. Below is the name of the service, the media used (found in parenthesis), and the speed of the service.

Table 2-2. WAN Speeds

Name	Speed
Standard phone wire (twisted pair)	9.6kb, 14.4kb, 28.8kb
DS0—Switched 56 (twisted pair)	64kb
ISDN—BRI (twisted pair)	128kb (2-64kb lines)
DS1—T1 (fiber optics) (24 DS0 lines)	1.544Mb
OC1-DS3-T3 (fiber optics) (28 T1 lines)	44.5Mb
OC3 (fiber optics)	155Mb
OC12 (fiber optics)	622Mb (12-51.84Mb lines)
OC48 (fiber optics)	2.4GB

(Digital signal (DS), Optical Carrier (OC), kb-Kilobit (1,024 bits), Mb-Megabits (1,0448,576 bits), GB = Gigabytes, 8 bits make 1 byte, 1 byte = 1 character)

Local Area Networks

There are three types of local area network topologies found today: bus, ring, and star.

Bus

Bus technology also is referred to as CSMA/CD (carrier sense multiple access/collision detect). On a bus network, all

Figure 2-3. Bus Network

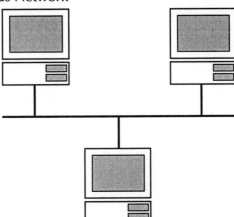

nodes (communications devices) are connected directly to the network. The data link layer of the protocol manages the following process: All the nodes listen on the network. If a node wants to send information, it listens to make sure no one else is sending information. If the line is clear, it sends the information. To receive information, all the nodes listen on the network to see if information with their name is being sent. Sometimes two nodes may listen, hear nothing, and simultaneously send information. When both nodes send information simultaneously, a collision occurs. The sending station detects this collision and sends a jam signal to all the nodes on the network. Both nodes back off for a randomly selected time period before attempting to retransmit. If subsequent attempts also result in a collision, the node continues to back off and retry up to fifteen times before giving up. At that point, the user is notified that the send failed. Bus technologies are simple to use, easy to install, and inexpensive. They tend to be reliable; if one node "falls off," all other nodes continue operating. Having too many nodes on the same network may result in collisions and delays. Xerox's Ethernet uses a bus-based technology.

Ring

Ring technologies connect each node to its neighbor node. All nodes have a table identifying the name of the other nodes on the network. When a node wants to send a message, it sends the message to its neighbor. The neighbor looks to see if the message is addressed to it. If not, the node passes the information to its neighbor node. A token-passing network passes a frame or token around the ring. Any network can have token passing. Nodes can only transmit information when they have the token. Dual-ring networks allow two simultaneous networks or a backup network to be used. Ring networks tend to be more expensive than bus networks. Token rings don't have collisions but will fail if any segment in the ring is disconnected. IBM's Token Ring and FDDI (dual ring network) are examples of token ring networks.

Figure 2-4. Ring Network

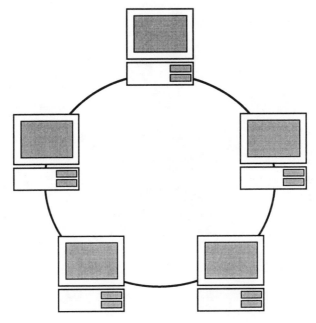

Star

In a star network, every node is connected to a central server. The central server has all the intelligence. Nodes send information to the central server. The central server then sends the information to the destination node. Star networks may be expensive because there must be a computer dedicated to managing the network. Upgrades also tend to be expensive because each workstation needs to be wired into this central computer. If a central server node goes out, the network can go out unless a backup path has been provided. Star networks are usually very reliable and safe, however, since there is an intelligent central server. IBM's mainframe Systems Network Architecture (SNA) and ATM use star technology.

Wide Area Networks

WANs can be point-to-point, multipoint, or multicast. Point-to-point networks allow one device to connect directly to another

Figure 2-5. Star Network

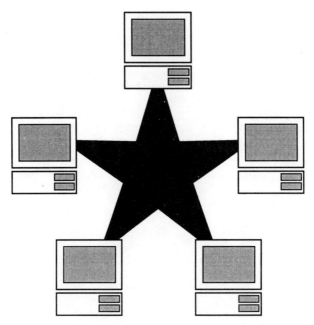

device using a WAN service provider. Multipoint networks allow a single connection from one station to fan out to several locations. This type of configuration can be used to minimize costs on long-distance lines to remote but clustered locations. Multicast networks are not a line but a packet or frame destination. The sender will send out a packet or frame (units of information), but instead of sending to a specific address at a certain station, or to a broadcast address at every station, a multicast broadcast is accepted by every station in that multicast group.

WAN Protocols

WAN data link protocols describe how frames of information are carried between systems on a single data link. These protocols are designed to operate over dedicated point-to-point facilities and multipoint facilities based on dedicated facilities and multiaccess switched services such as Frame Relay. The main WAN protocols are SDLC, PPP, LAPB, and HDLC.

Figure 2-6. WAN Networks

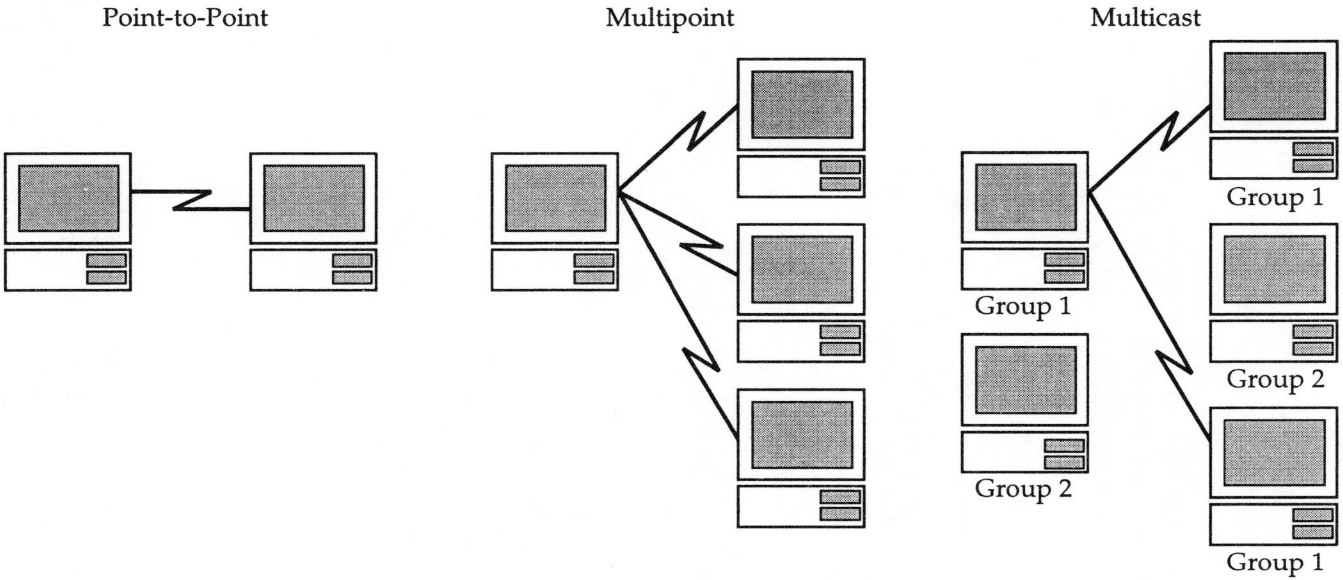

Point-to-Point

Multipoint

Multicast

Group 1

Group 2

Group 1

Group 1

Group 2

Synchronous Data Link Control (SDLC) is IBM's WAN protocol. SDLC defines a multipoint WAN environment that allows several devices to connect to a dedicated facility.

Point-to-Point Protocol (PPP) was developed by the Internet Engineering Task Force. PPP contains a protocol field to identify the network layer protocol. Unlike HDLC, the protocol field of PPP is standardized, allowing different vendors' products to be internetworked.

Link Access Procedures Balance (LAPB) is primarily used with X.25 standards networks but can be used as a simple data link transport. LAPB includes capabilities for detecting out-of-sequence or missing frames, as well as exchanging, retransmitting, and acknowledging frames.

High-Level Data Link Control (HDLC) is the International Standards Organization (ISO) standard. HDLC supports both point-to-point and multipoint configurations.

Logical Link Control (LLC) adds sequencing and reliability to a single linked line. LLC's main function is to multiplex between network layer protocols, for example, between IP and DECnet.

LAN and WAN Technologies

Currently there are many companies that provide products based on the following LAN and WAN technologies.

Table 2-3. LAN Technologies

Technology	Protocol	Speed
Ethernet	Bus—CSMA/CD	10Mb or 100Mb
Token Ring	Token Ring	4Mb or 16Mb
FDDI	Token Ring	100Mb
ATM	Star	52Mb, 155Mb

Ethernet is a ubiquitous bus-based technology. It is easy to administrate and simple to use. Ethernet sends information in large frames, allowing data to be passed rapidly between nodes. A node can be taken off the network without any effect to other nodes. Large Ethernet networks may have collisions.

ATM uses a network star topology. Each secondary node is connected into a central node. Stars can be intertwined by having secondary nodes act as central nodes to another star. ATM's frame sizes are always 5-byte headers with 48 bytes of data. This small format makes ATM efficient in sending voice, data, and video.

Table 2-4. WAN Technologies

Type	Technology	Speed/Lines
Standard phone service	Switched circuit	Up to 28.8kb (new modems support 33.6kb)
ISDN	Switched circuit: Special phone service that allows higher speeds over standard twisted pair	128kb using 2-56kb lines
Dedicated line (freeway phones)	Dedicated line	Up to 28.8kb
X.25	Variable packet size, slow, inefficient, developed for old, noisy switching equipment	56kb
Frame relay	Variable packet size, fast, efficient, developed for clean fiber lines	T1
SMDS	Cell-based technology, Bell Corp's very fast proprietary network	T3
ATM	Cell-based technology, fast, flexible	52Mb, 155Mb, 622Mb, 2,400Mb

Hardware That Connects Networks

The following types of hardware serve as connectors.

Figure 2-7. Repeater

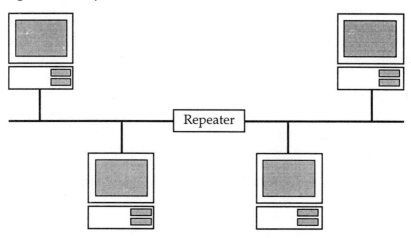

Repeaters

Repeaters extend networks by interconnected segments. Repeaters are unintelligent. They receive, amplify, and retime signals. The benefit of repeaters is that they are an inexpensive way to increase the length of a network. The downside is that since they amplify signals, they may amplify faulty signals and errors.

Multiplexers

Multiplexers combine one or more input channels into one or more output channels. Multiplexing increases the utilization of the physical media by sharing it among more than one source of traffic. *Time division multiplexing* (TDM) is often used. There are three major classes of TDM:

- Fixed—The output channel is divided into fixed time slots that are assigned to each input channel. This dedicates bandwidth on the input channel even when there isn't any traffic.

Figure 2-8. Multiplexers

- Statistical—Time slot assignments are made dynamically.
- Isochronous—Combines the dynamic aspects of the statistical multiplexer with fixed-size time slots to provide guaranteed throughput.

Hubs

A hub is an active physical layer device. Hubs are most often used to connect the wiring closet to the desktop. Each user station is wired to a hub in the nearest wiring closet, thereby creating a physical star network. The hub has evolved from being a dumb wiring concentrator to an intelligent switching device that can route traffic. Intelligent switches send data to a designated port. Without switch technology data are broadcast to all ports. Two types of hub-based configurations are commonly used:

- Distributed backbone: Hubs are used primarily as a LAN concentration device; routers are located on each floor.
- Collapsed backbone: Hubs are located on each floor, with routers located by the building entrance.

Bridges

A bridge is designed to interconnect LANs to form the appearance of a single larger network. Bridges have become more intel-

Figure 2-9. Hubs

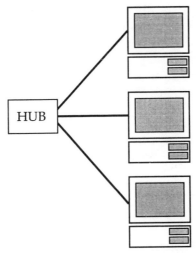

Figure 2-10. Bridges

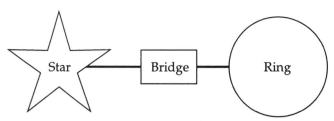

ligent. They now filter traffic by (MAC—i.e., media access control) address or by protocol type; traffic is not unnecessarily circulated throughout the internetwork.

Routers

Routers are active and intelligent network nodes. Typically they are employed to support multiple protocol stack environments. They can participate in managing the network, providing dynamic control over resources and supporting engineering and maintenance activities. Routers incorporate bridging functions and may serve as a limited form of hub.

What Is TCP/IP?

TCP/IP is one of the protocol stacks discussed earlier in this chapter. TCP/IP *(Transmission Control Protocol/ Internet Protocol)* is the common name for a family of data communications protocols used to organize computers and data communications equipment into computer networks. In the context of the Internet TCP/IP manages the flow of information from one com-

Figure 2-11. Routers

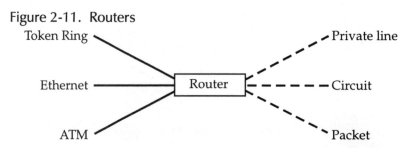

puter to another computer. TCP/IP was developed by the U.S. Department of Defense to interconnect hosts on ARPANET, PRNET (packet radio), and SATNET (packet satellite). All three of these networks have since been retired. TCP/IP has grown in use, since it is very flexible. Because of this flexibility TCP/IP can be found on almost every kind of computer.

TCP/IP is at the core of the Internet. A group of Internet Protocol (IP) applications are run on each Internet server. The basis of IP is a management system that gives each computer on the Internet a unique address. Anyone can apply for a unique Internet address; it is relatively inexpensive and takes about six weeks to receive this unique address. The unique address is managed by the IP layer. This number is used by the IP protocol to allow hosts and workstations to communicate with each other. A computer on the Internet is continually polling major Internet sites to make sure the sites are working and can receive information. The IP application on the computer maintains a log of all IP addresses known to that computer. The log information maintained by the computer is the unique IP address converted from the name we see to a number that is easier for a computer to manage. The computer turns this log into a routing table.

Specifically a computer attached to the Internet uses IP commands to poll the network. Each computer connected to the Internet has a list of closely located computers saved in a routing table that is continually updated. This table maps the network topology by storing how far away the network is and which router the computer next needs to send a packet to in order to reach a network not directly connected. A utility called *address resolution protocol* (ARP) is the actual mechanism responsible for mapping IP addresses to physical addresses. If a server is moved, ARP finds the new location and changes this location in its table. This way clients do not need to know where sites are located or how to get to a site.

The TCP segment of the protocol makes sure commands get through to the other end. TCP keeps track of what is sent, and retransmits anything that did not get through. If any text is too large for one datagram (the text being sent), TCP will split it up into several datagrams and make sure that all the datagrams arrive correctly.

(Text continues on page 29.)

Figure 2-12. IP Routing

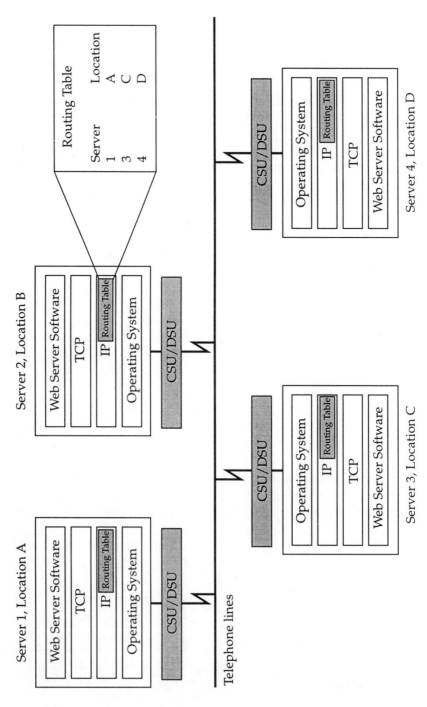

Figure 2-13. Datagram Routing

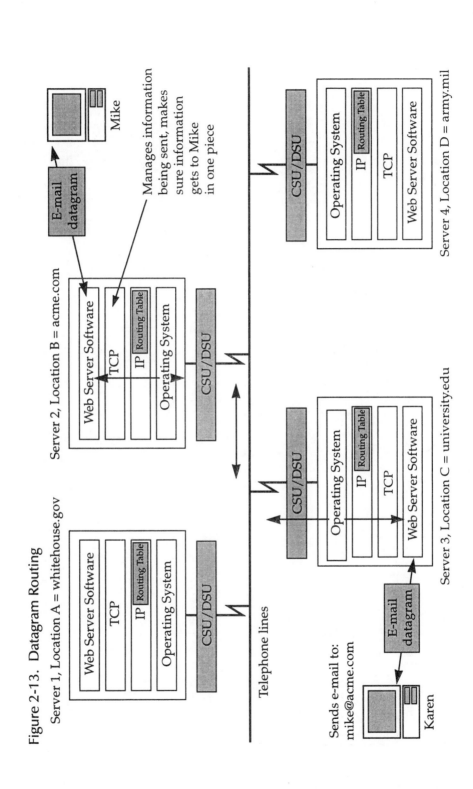

Figure 2-14. IP Hierarchy

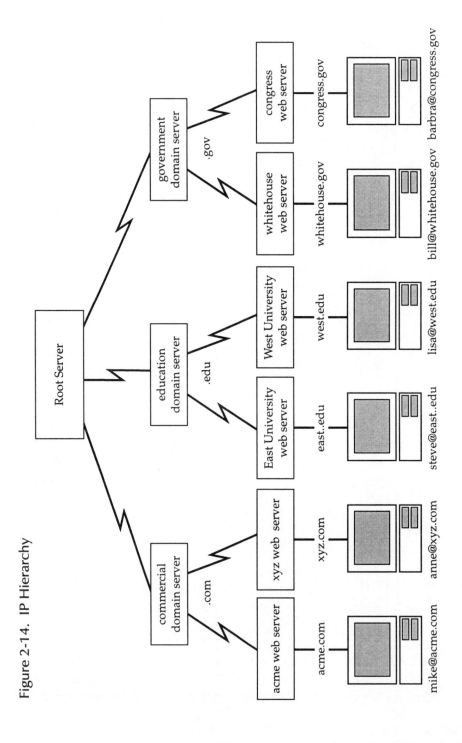

Within TCP/IP there is a hierarchy of servers. A *root server* is at the top of the hierarchy, next a *domain server*, then the *local server*, and finally the *client*. Clients are limited by the size of connection of the servers they need to go through. For instance, a client might have fast access to any information within his local server, but might have slow access when getting information at the domain level. This slow access is a sign to the web master to increase the bandwidth of the network connection between the local server and the domain. The same might apply to domain servers. Clients might have fast access to local sites and sites within their domain. Servers might be slow when accessing information outside of their domain. The web master then needs to petition the organization that manages their domain to increase network bandwidth. Clients in international sites accessing information within their country's domain might not have any problem, though access outside of their country's domain might be slow. This will show up if the client attempts to download information or access a site located in another country's domain or in a domain like *com, edu,* or *gov.* Slow access between international domains might be harder to change since increasing bandwidth takes getting a country's government to increase their network environment. Web masters servicing international sites need to track international domains that have slow access. If the international domain is a potential source of large revenue, the company might want to put a mirrored site in that country. A *mirrored site* is a computer running a copy of your Internet site within the other country's domain. With a mirrored site local residents don't need to go out of their domain to access your company's information.

Internet Terminology

Anonymous FTP Supports sending and receiving files from host computers using the identification "anonymous." Anonymous FTP (File Transfer Protocol) is used to distribute software and information. Anonymous FTP is a convention for setting up guest accounts with file transfer capability. The name "anonymous" is issued as the ID and an Internet mailing address is used as the password.

API (Application Program Interface) A specification that is laid out to explain to a programmer how to write code and have the code successfully work with the product.

Applets Small programs that can be downloaded or run from a web browser. People running a web browser can download and run an applet on their computer. Downloaded applets run faster and use less system resources than a full application.

Archie An information system that supports anonymous FTP. Archie offers an electronic directory service for locating files and documents on the Internet.

CGI (Common Gateway Interface) The Internet standard interface for invoking server-based scripts or compiled programs at the request of a client. CGI is an interface used to create interactive applications within a web site. An example of a CGI application is a stock trading report. With a stock trading report a client can enter a company's stock identifier into a web screen and the current trading rate of that company is displayed.

Client The generic name for any person or computer accessing a computer.

Cookies A mechanism (program) placed on a client computer by a server application that allows the server application to store and retrieve information from the client. For example, the user name and password can be stored in a cookie so that clients don't have to enter their information as they navigate through protected locations on a web site; the server can automatically access the cookie to see if the client is allowed access to a location.

CSU/DSU Network equipment used at higher speeds to connect computers to communication services.

DNS (Domain Name System) A distributed database that maps the name of a computer to an IP address. DNS enables TCP/IP users to access network services by specifying the name of the computer they wish to connect to instead of its numeric address.

Electronic Mail (E-mail)   With e-mail address anyone can send messages to and receive them from anyone else who has an e-mail address. Internet mail is based on the *Simple Mail Transfer Protocol* (SMTP). The general format for a mail address is "user. name@location.domain".

Extranet   Intranet that allows people outside the organization to access information (may also be referred to as an Internet with password protection).

File Transfer Protocol (FTP)   Allows a user on any computer to get files from another computer, or to send files to another computer. FTP is a utility that can be run any time you want to access a file on another system. The file is downloaded to your computer and you can then use the information on your computer. Files can be secured. If you don't want anyone else downloading files on your computer, you can add security by requiring the user to specify a user name and password. FTP is a non-hardware specific utility; provisions are built into FTP for handling file transfers between different kinds of computers.

Fire Wall   A computer/router placed between the company's computer network and the Internet. All Internet access and e-mails pass through the fire wall, which checks for viruses and grants access.

Gopher   The Internet Gopher protocol is designed for distributed document search and retrieval. Gopher is an information service that provides users with convenient access to documents, databases, and campus information services.

HTML (Hyper Text Markup Language)   A programming language that is read by web browser and can display information in an easily readable way.

HTTP (Hyper Text Transport Protocol)   The standard protocol for communication between clients and servers on the WWW.

Internet   By using the same protocol, clients located around the world can communicate with each other and access common computer screens.

Intranet   Computers located throughout a company or organization that anyone within that company or organization can access.

JAVA A program language created by Sun Microsystems that can run on any computer. Java stuffs a lot of information into a little bit of code, making it perfect for the Internet, since people do not want to download large files.

JavaScript Similar to Java, JavaScript is a scripting language that allows dynamic behavior to be specified within html documents.

LDAP (Lightweight Directory Access Protocol) A protocol that makes it easier to locate names of users by their e-mail address. LDAP is a simplification of the X.500 *directory access protocol* (DAP).

LISTSERV An automated system for maintaining discussion lists. ListR supports services that allow people to read or post information to a chat line.

Livemedia An open architecture for handling real-time data, such as audio and video, over the Internet.

Netfind A simple Internet white pages directory facility. Given the name of a person on the Internet and a rough description of where the person works, Netfind attempts to locate telephone and electronic mailbox information about the person.

News Groups (USENET) Bulletin boards that allow users to read and respond to various topics. USENET is the set of machines that exchange articles tagged with one or more universally recognized labels, called news groups (or groups for short).

Ping (Packet Internet Groper) Ping tests the Internet to see what systems are working. Ping can also test and record the response time of accessing other computers. This provides a systems administrator with valuable information on what networks are overloaded so they can optimize access times.

Plug-Ins Programs that can be bought or downloaded that provide added functionality. Plug-ins plug into a browser and can be run by a client's computer.

Publish The process of moving files to an Internet/intranet site. Once published, files can be viewed by anyone who has access to that site.

Talk Supports direct writing to another user. Talk is a visual communications program that copies lines from your terminal directly to the terminal of another user. People can use this connection to type messages back and forth in real time.

Telnet (Network Terminal Protocol) (also called remote login). Telnet allows a user to log in on any computer on the network. A user in California can access and use a computer in New York. It will appear as if he is actually working in New York.

Remote execution Requests can be made to run a program on a remote computer. Remote execution is useful when most of your work is on a small computer, but a few tasks require the resources of a larger system.

Remote printing Allows someone to access printers on another computer as if the remote printer were located locally. If a business has a large production printer, employees can access the production printer directly from their desk using remote printing.

URL (Universal Resource Locator) Information used by the computer to find the page requested. For example, the URL for finding Netscape would be the http://home.netscape.com

Server A computer that hosts an application or web site.

Veronica (Very Easy Rodent-Oriented Netwide Index to Computerized Archives) Veronica supports Gopher applications by indexing information on servers. With Veronica, Gopher does not have to search every system and every menu each time a Gopher search is started.

VRML (Virtual Reality Modeling Language) A modeling language for creating three-dimensional information through which users can navigate. Three-dimensional information ranges from games to complex analysis.

WAIS (Wide Area Information Servers) A distributed information retrieval system. Helps users search databases over networks using an easy-to-use interface. The databases (called *sources*) are mostly collections of text-based documents, but they may also contain sound, pictures, or video as well.

Web Browser Graphical user interface (GUI) lets people access the Internet using graphics, drag-and-drop, and point-and-click features. A good browser can support applets and other features called plug-ins.

Web Editor   The person responsible for managing the content of a web site.

Web Master   The person responsible for managing the technology (applications, addresses) of a web site.

WWW (World Wide Web)   A worldwide, interconnected system of servers that offers information in hypertext format. World Wide Web is an information system based on hypertext, which offers a means of moving from document to document (usually called *navigating*) within a network of information.

How All This Technology Fits Into the Internet/Intranet

Client-Server Model

Most recently the computing world has been organized into the client-server model. The client-server model consists of a three-layer architecture. The bottom layer consists of workstations, typically PCs. The PC or client is where the person resides. PCs are locally connected to each other using a LAN. PCs are grouped, usually by location or function, to a departmental server. The departmental server lets the PCs in a work group share facilities like modems, faxes, printers, or databases. The local server connects to a corporate server. The corporate server stores corporate information. Corporate information might be company financials, inventory, or the customer database. A company might have many corporate servers, each storing one type of information.

Large companies with offices located in many countries might decide to have mirrored servers to support employees on different continents. For instance, an office in Boston might have twenty employees. All the employees share one local server. When an employee needs access to corporate records on a customer, the local server calls up the corporate computer in New York. The same architecture would work for an employee in En-

Figure 2-15. Client Server Model

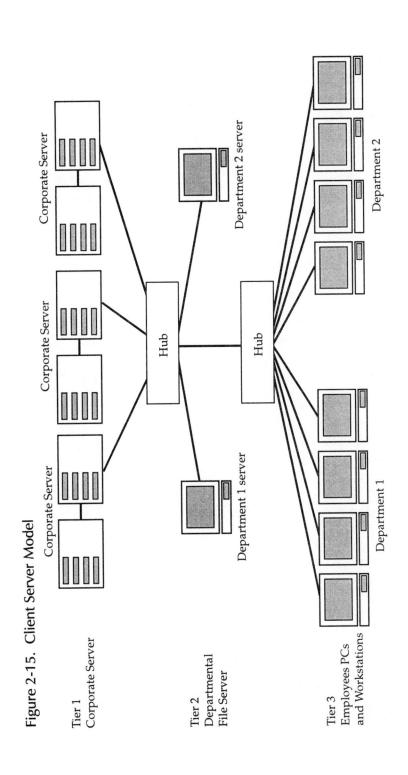

Tier 1
Corporate Server

Corporate Server

Corporate Server

Corporate Server

Hub

Department 1 server

Hub

Tier 2
Departmental
File Server

Department 2 server

Department 2

Department 1

Tier 3
Employees PCs
and Workstations

Figure 2-16. Intraoffice Communication

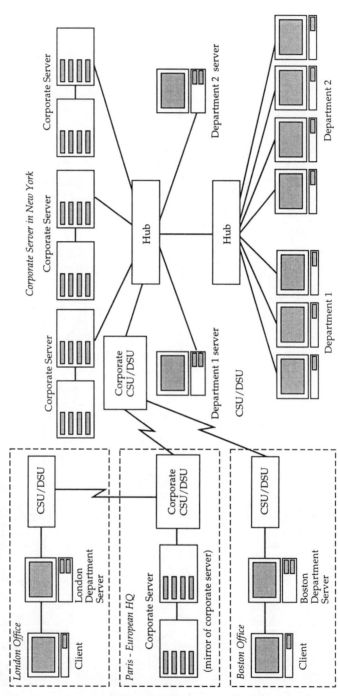

gland. Instead of calling a computer in New York it might be less expensive and faster to call the corporate computer in France. The corporate computer in France and the one in New York would talk to each other and have the same information (a mirrored site). Earlier in the chapter it was explained how the computers talk to each other locally (LAN) and remotely (WAN).

Product Backgrounder

There are many good applications on the market that support Internet applications. In this book we will use some of Netscape's applications for our examples. Netscape was chosen because Netscape is the largest provider of Internet infrastructure technology. Outlined below are the core Netscape applications that are needed in order to create basic web site services. Applications that provide finer-grained management, specialized management, or specialty applications like meeting scheduling are available but not included in this backgrounder. To find out more about the latest web services and applications, visit the sites of web software companies. The three largest providers of web software are Netscape, IBM, and Microsoft. Each company's site has in-depth details on their latest offerings and nicely articulated case studies showing how companies have used their technologies. Netscape, IBM, and Microsoft can each be found on the Internet at the following addresses, respectively:

http://www.netscape.com
http://www.ibm.com
http://www.microsoft.com

Another good place to find information on the latest web applications is the newsstand. Computer magazines periodically rank the top applications and run articles on applications features and functionality.

Following is a list of the Netscape applications this book will use in the examples:

Client Software (Connects your workstation to the Internet.)

- Navigator Graphical user interface placed on employees' workstations so they can access Internet/intranet applications.

- Navigator Gold Extension, which supports easy creation of html documents.

Server Software (If you are not using an ISP, you will need server software.)

- FastTrack web server software—infrastructure software needed to attach to the Internet. Supports Java and Java-Script for publishing traditional Internet documents.
- Enterprise web server software—infrastructure software needed to attach to the Internet. Enterprise is a more feature-enhanced version of FastTrack. This includes more tools for server management, content creation, management, development, and performance.
- News server software that provides the infrastructure for news groups. If you create a news forum, or chat line, you will need a server to manage this facility.
- Mail server software that provides the infrastructure for electronic mail. If you provide e-mail you will need a server to manage transfer, storage, and accessing of e-mail. To increase speed, mail servers should be located throughout your organization.
- Catalog server software that provides clients with the ability to find resources, both information and people. Catalog tracks all information on the Internet or intranet. Clients access the catalog screen and input the subject they are searching; then the catalog identifies all places that information is located.
- Proxy server software for replicating and filtering web content. Proxy saves popular documents so clients can access the document without having to access the network. Proxy can also be configured to limit access (the company can decide what kinds of web sites users can access).
- LiveWirePro server software that provides a connection between the Internet content and database applications. If you are writing CGI applications, there is a good chance you will need to access your corporate databases. Live-WirePro provides the infrastructure to develop and support applications that access your internal databases.

- SuiteSpot—the family name of Netscape's server products.

Transaction Software (Runs a store on the Internet.)

- LivePayment—virtual point-of-sale terminal (encrypted credit card processing functions).
- Merchant server—provides infrastructure for a virtual store, including product information for browsing and purchase selection, product search, promotional discounts, flexible pricing, dynamic product displays, and multimedia integration capabilities. Transaction support includes processing, shipping, sales tax charges, and secure order delivery.

Intranet technology consists of a group of applications using client-server technology. A company with an intranet would put a web browser on each of the employees' PCs. The client's server computer would then have access to the company's intranet web site computer (Enterprise). The local office would have a mail and proxy server (this can be an office physically located in a different city or a different building). Periodically (decided by IS) the proxy server will call up the central Enterprise server and download all the most-requested web pages. Having a proxy server saves time and network cost. The mail server will forward all mail in that office to the people located in the office and save the mail addressed to people not located locally.

Periodically (decided by IS) the mail server will call up the corporate mail server. All stored messages designated for people outside the location will be sent to the corporate mail server for distribution. Any mail messages intended for local clients will be downloaded to the local mail server and distributed to each client. Local clients needing access to applications outside the local office will go through the proxy server. The proxy server will figure out if a copy of the application was saved locally or if the proxy server needs to connect the client with another computer. If the information is not resident on the local proxy server, the local proxy server will decide if the client has permission to access the site

(Text continues on page 42.)

Figure 2-17. Intranet Communications

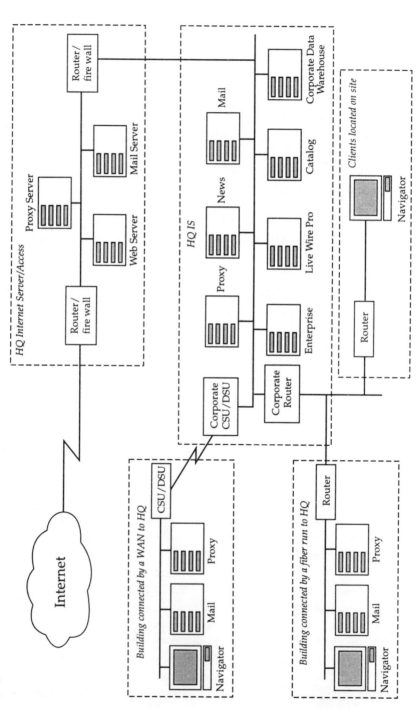

Figure 2-18. Catalog-Type Application Running on Yahoo

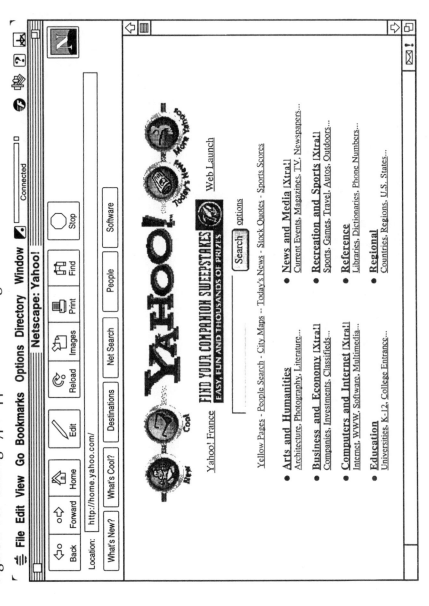

requested. The proxy server will then call up the corporate enterprise server, requesting access to the site. Clients request sites by either entering a URL location, clicking on an icon (clicking an icon transmits a URL location), or by running a query with catalog and clicking on a location displayed by catalog.

Internet clients can either access the Internet through their company's enterprise server or the company can farm out Internet access to an ISP (Internet service provider). The most popular ISP (by clients served) is America Online (AOL). Clients install the AOL browser on their computer. They then call up AOL. AOL connects them to the AOL web page, or clients can access the WWW. AOL's services are focused on the home user. Businesses and organizations want their ISP to focus services on their needs. The type of services businesses and organizations want are home site creation, employee access to the Internet by using standard browsers, ability to block access to certain web sites, e-mail support, and an Internet name server address for e-mail (employee@name server. domain). Most ISPs can provide business services.

To find out more on how to decide what services are right for your company and how to create an Internet/intranet business case, read Chapter 3.

3

Is an Internet/ Intranet Right for My Company?

Where to Start

The starting point for most Internets or intranets is the *home page*. A home page is the first screen people see when signing on to your web site. Companies, organizations, and individuals have created their own home pages. Home pages can be used to inform others about your company; provide information on services, products, or job offerings; or be the central place to find out the latest information. A home page is the central "meeting place" for web users accessing your site. It is the starting point for any application you want a client to access.

Internet and Intranet Applications Can Be Active or Passive

Passive home pages are viewed but do not require anyone to do anything. These tend to be easier web sites to build, since you need to provide only content (the information you read). For example, intranet web sites can have a passive home page that tells employees more about the company. A company's public relations department can post press releases, human resources can post information on discrimination laws or medical plans, marketing can post the latest data sheets and information on the competition, and sales can post the latest "big deal." Internet users who are looking for a new car can look up car companies and view specifications about available cars, see pictures of the car, or run a movie showing the car moving. Real estate agencies are putting house listings on the web with location, specifications, floor plans, and pictures of the house.

Active home pages allow clients to do more than view. Clients can post comments to a company's chat line saying what they think about the product. If he is interested in buying a product, a client can read other clients' postings. You too can use the Internet to support vendors or customers. Customers running a browser can access your data through a password, or you can provide open access to anyone. An applet is a section of an application that is downloaded and run on a client's computer. By developing applets, people who access your home page can download an applet and then run the applet on their computer using your computer to access your data. The benefit of this client-server approach is that an application run on a client computer will be faster. Movies or cartoons run on the client computer won't use as much of your network or computer bandwidth, allowing you to support more simulations sessions.

An example of an active site for an instrument company is an Internet application that supports instrument maintenance. The instrument company can provide an applet to service technicians. The applet lets the company's technicians perform periodic tests to make sure the company's instruments are correctly calibrated. Since the applet runs on a PC, the technician can use already available technology to hook up the PC to the instrument, run the test, receive feedback, and, at a later, more convenient time, upload the information to the company. The company can now use this information for statistical research. If the company finds a common problem they can notify the technicians by sending an e-mail message. If they ascertain that the problem is caused by poor training, they can produce a movie or create a moving illustration that highlights the proper way to maintain or install the instrument. The movie or illustration can be accessed and downloaded through the same browser interface that the technician uses to test the diagnostics. A movie plug-in on the technicians' computer will allow them to run the

Figure 3-1. Passive Web Site

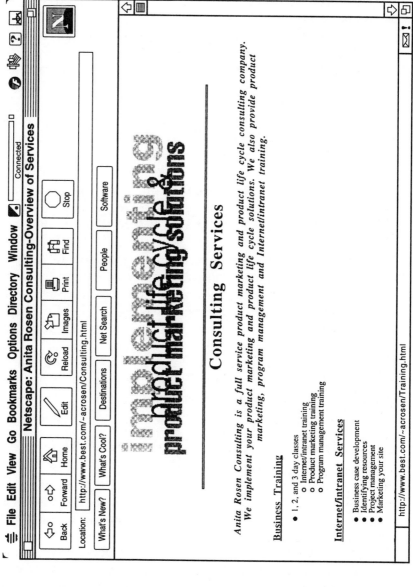

File Edit View Go Bookmarks Options Directory Window

Netscape: Anita Rosen Consulting-Overview of Services

| Back | Forward | Home | Reload | Images | Print | Find | Stop |

Location: http://www.best.com/~acrosen/Consulting.html

| What's New? | What's Cool? | Destinations | Net Search | People | Software |

Consulting Services

Anita Rosen Consulting is a full service product marketing and product life cycle consulting company. We implement your product marketing and product life cycle solutions. We also provide product marketing, program management and Internet/intranet training.

Business Training

- 1, 2, and 3 day classes
  - Internet/intranet training
  - Product marketing training
  - Program management training

Internet/Intranet Services

- Business case development
- Identifying resources
- Project management
- Marketing your site

http://www.best.com/~acrosen/Training.html

movie at their convenience. Internet technology uses the same philosophy used in conventional client-server technology. The difference between applications developed conventionally and with Internet technology is that browser applications are universal and inexpensive.

Transaction-type applications work well on the Internet/intranet. Currently many software companies allow people to try out their software by allowing free downloads (FTP). Transportation services, like buses, trains, and airlines, allow people to access schedules and book tickets. By accessing the site of a transportation service, you can find out schedule times and prices. Tickets can be purchased by entering arrival and departure locations, times, and dates and then entering your credit card information when the trip you want is available. Courier companies like UPS and Federal Express let you track your packages through a web interface, find pricing, or ask questions. Financial institutions let you track your portfolio, view statements, and transfer money. Specific applications can be written for specialized situations; applets can be created to support fieldwork. For example, a quote-and-proposal system for salespeople can be developed. Salespeople can create complicated proposals while in the field without having to access host systems. The latest terms and conditions can be automatically downloaded to sales computers, ensuring accurate proposals. Training movies or an executive interview can be sent to a remote office's file server using FTP. Employees can run these movies on their PC using a movie plug-in.

How to Choose What Type of Site You Should Have

The first step in creating a successful site is to figure out why you want to create an Internet/intranet site. Don't play games with yourself. Be honest about your reason. You need to fully understand your motivation so you don't sabotage your own plan. If you think having an Internet site would be cool for your company, understand why you think it would be cool. If you want to have an Internet site because you want to be a web mas-

Figure 3-2. Active Web Site

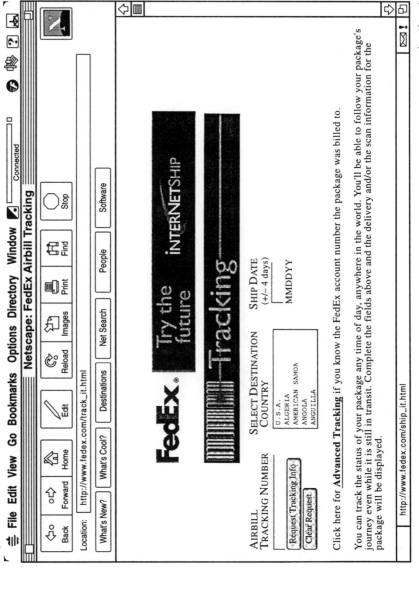

(continues)

Figure 3-2. (continued)

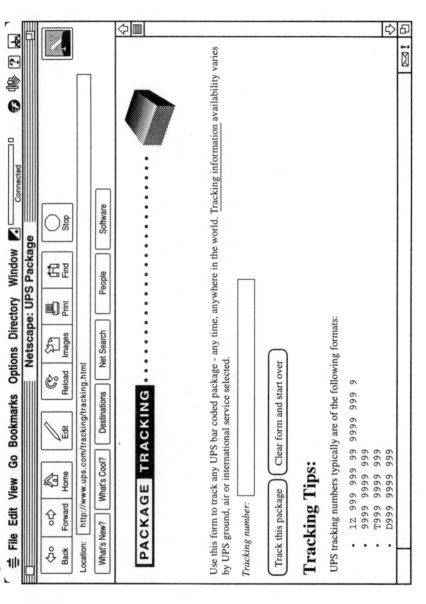

File Edit View Go Bookmarks Options Directory Window

Netscape: UPS Package

Connected

| Back | Forward | Home | Edit | Reload | Images | Print | Find | Stop |

Location: http://www.ups.com/tracking/tracking.html

| What's New? | What's Cool? | Destinations | Net Search | People | Software |

PACKAGE TRACKING •

Use this form to track any UPS bar coded package - any time, anywhere in the world. Tracking information availability varies by UPS ground, air or international service selected.

Tracking number:

[Track this package] [Clear form and start over]

Tracking Tips:

UPS tracking numbers typically are of the following formats:

- 1Z 999 999 99 9999 999 9
- 9999 9999 999
- T999 9999 999
- D999 9999 999

ter, understand this motivation up front. Your motivation may be because you think the company will miss the boat if they don't have a site. All of these are valid reasons for developing a business case. You can make intelligent decisions if you understand your own motivation. People can read hidden agendas, and they make them feel uncomfortable. If your agenda is open, it frees you to make intelligent choices.

The next step is to create a successful business case that will get budget approval. You will need to clearly articulate your goal and plan. Step one in creating a successful plan is to write down the hottest topics your management organization has. Hot topics might be market share, worker productivity, fast customer support, access to new markets, revenue per employee, speed to market, cost cutting, or productivity increases. All executives have at least one topic they are obsessed with. Once you identify this topic, you have the theme for your site. Don't let knowledge cloud your judgment. You might have spent the last year surfing the web and you might know a lot of great web applications that would benefit your company. The goal of this exercise is to get your business plan approved. Once you have established a successful web site, you can increase the web applications on your site. Initially focus on one goal; don't muddy the waters by giving executive staff too much information. Keep your plan simple. Focus on the goal, and think of ways a web site would help actualize the goal. Surf the Internet and visualize what the goal is of each of the sites you visit.

The table on page 50 presents a list of goals, along with an explanation of why a web site would actualize those goals.

The goal and solution have to be tailored to your company. Once you identify the hot topic and web solution, you need to figure out what kind of infrastructure you will need to support this solution. How much will this site cost? What potential revenue can you expect to receive from this site? Once you establish your site's goal and figure out how an Internet will let you actualize this goal, you can figure out what kind of content you will need to create to fulfill the requirements of the site. Take the time now to write down any hot topics you know executives at your company are concerned with. Is this concern an internal or external concern? If it is an internal concern, you will probably

Table 3-1. Goal/Solution

Company Goal	Web Solution
Increase market share	Web site is global; provides access to larger market
Increase worker productivity	Customers can access the web site to get information instead of having to speak to a real person
Access to new markets	Global web site can be targeted at new market
Increase revenue per employee	Selling on the web may create a shorter sales cycle
Increase speed to market	Jump-start distribution cycle by advertising product the same day as available
Cut costs	Automating a process may save money
Increase productivity	Accessing information on-line may save time

be building an intranet business case. If it is an external concern, you will probably be building an Internet site.

How to Choose an Internet/Intranet Application

Many internal applications in use today can be easily supported using an intranet. Human resources applications like job information, name and phone number lists, and medical benefits can all be displayed on an HR web page. A finance web site might display information on time cards, expense reports, or credit authorization. Having the information accessible on a server lets the employees know that they can easily access the latest information. E-mail and chat lines can be set up to facilitate communications. Meeting minutes can be sent electronically to distribution lists. Employees can easily archive meeting minutes, accessing them at their own convenience. Providing access to applications for customers might save your company money and provide increased services to customers. For example, a modular furniture company might want to provide Internet access to their design system to large customers. Customers may input their customer ID and password. They then will be asked to identify what building and what floor. An existing diagram of the building's layout will be displayed. Customers can then reconfigure their office layout. The furniture company does not have to send a person to the site to help with every design question.

How to Know If an Internet/Intranet Is for You

Having a goal and visualizing a way to accomplish that goal have to be tempered with the reality of understanding your targeted client. Before you start you need to ask yourself a few basic questions. If you say yes to these questions, an Internet/intranet might be a good bet for your company:

Does the target client have access to a computer? This is one of the most important questions you need to ask. If the people you are targeting do not have a computer, developing a business case will probably be beyond the scope of what you can do. For instance, if a large national store is thinking of using an intranet to disseminate information to their salespeople but the salespeople never have access to a computer, the program will fail. On the other hand, if the application is for store managers who already have a PC on their desk, an intranet could be a success. Following are some applications that might be successful for this national chain: The store's headquarters might want to send pictures of successful store displays or run an applet at the store manager's desk that allows the manager to optimize employee work schedules. E-mail might be sent daily, highlighting what products go on sale. Chat lines might facilitate answers for management issues like employee problems or slow-moving product lines. Managers can post successes or post questions to other store managers on the chat line. Other managers who have faced similar problems can help solve problems. Management can keep track of issues, quickly identifying common concerns and creating programs to assist employees.

Can you reuse the current infrastructure? Are you looking at developing an application that many people within the company will use? One of the outstanding features of Internet technology is it reuses existing infrastructure. Internet applications are less expensive to buy and develop than the same product in a non-Internet version. If you are looking at developing a new application, it is worthwhile to find out whether developing this technology using Internet/intranet technology would work. Many computer software companies are creating Internet/intranet versions of their product for ten percent of the cost of their standard product. Applets and plug-ins are easy ways to create new applications. Internet/intranet applications can be created with nice visuals that are easy for clients to use.

Can you identify an application that will save you money if automated? Can you identify current cost centers in which an intranet solution will work? For instance, perhaps the HR department mails out a benefits package to each employee at a cost of $10 each ($2 for mailing, $8 for printing). Depending on how many employees you have, it might be cheaper to put the information up on the web. Employees can view the information through the home page, and they can print out the information locally. The savings on postage alone might justify the cost of developing the application on an intranet. Below is a list of applications companies have automated for their intranet.

budget planning	facilities management
call tracking	presentation library
contract library	product catalog
room reservation	contest results
call dispatch system	suggestion box
events calendar	equipment inventory
expense report	travel authorization
financial research	objective and key result
job postings	listing
purchasing tracking	help desk access
industry news	401k and employee stock
patient treatment sign-off	purchase program

time cards
training schedule
proposal planning
meeting minutes
interdepartmental project
    discussions
sales order entry and
    tracing

budget status
on-line training
competitive data
press releases
order tracking
order placement
customer information

Defining Product Concept Direction

Write down your idea for using an Internet/intranet as clearly as possible. Writing down the idea helps cement the thought and provides a good audit trail. If this is an existing application and employees have been asking for additional functionality, you could:

- Poll employees and create a document that identifies the feature/functionality input received
- Identify reasons why this new application would be beneficial to the company
- Identify at whom the application is targeted
- Identify potential cost savings

If you are creating this application because of a merger, you could include in the document a section identifying:

- What the current technology situation(s) is
- What possible direction(s) the company may take

For a new application idea you could write down:

- What the concept is
- Who this concept will benefit
- How this concept will benefit them

Start simply; this does not need to be a thesis. An example for a concept statement for a company-wide e-mail program might be:

- *Concept:* Instituting a company-wide e-mail program.
- *Target:* Current workers who have daily access to computers.
- *Company benefit:* Saves money by decreasing the amount of paper and people needed to distribute interoffice memos. Increases productivity, since employees get timely information. Increases intracompany communication, since employees can easily send and receive messages to each other. Decreases confusion, since there is an audit trail of messages sent and received.
- *Work-flow benefit:* Workers can now send messages from their desk and receive messages at their desk. Audit trails can now be created to ensure information is received. Information can be received in a timely fashion. Employees working different schedules or traveling can still maintain contact and manage processes. Memos that need to be sent to a large group can be easily sent from the author's desk without administrative intervention.

Recommendations for Choosing Projects

When an idea is presented it is a good policy to have a simple checklist to make sure the idea meets basic corporate requirements. The following is an example of this kind of list:

- Is the solution's ROI (return on investment) acceptable?
- Is the infrastructure created by this solution reusable?
- Can you use known technology to create this solution?
- Does the solution reuse infrastructure already created?
- Do people within the company's IS organization understand how to develop this kind of solution?
- How difficult will it be to retrain employees in this methodology?
- Is there easy access to new/future IS employees who can augment/support this type of application?

A Quick Look at Cost

Before a detailed analysis is done, a quick review of the product can be conducted to give you an idea if it is reasonable to consider this solution. Figure out how much it should cost to develop and implement the new application, how many employees will be affected over the next three years, and the product's average cost.

To get cost information call up local Internet service providers (ISPs). They will provide you with a full listing of their services. If you don't know any ISPs, buy a computer magazine that has an Internet article on the cover. The back of the magazine will have many ISP listings. Call the design firm you currently are doing business with. Find out if they are doing web design. Better yet, get yourself an Internet connection. Companies like AT&T or AOL have inexpensive, easy-to-connect offerings. Log on to a service like Alta Vista (www.altavista.digital.com) or Yahoo (www.yahoo.com). Run a search on ISP and Internet design. You will get pages of listings. You can visit the sites and view prices. Search sites that have applications similar to those you think your company would like. Send an e-mail to the site's web master (usually webmaster@sitename.domain will work). Tell the web master how much you like his site and explain what you are attempting to do. There is a good chance he will e-mail you back with some good information. Ask him to tell you how difficult it was to build the application and how long it took to create the application. Once you have some background information you can now figure out how much it will cost you to build a site. You can also use this as background reference information when presenting your plan. Questions you will need to answer are:

1. How many employees will be affected?
2. What is the cost of technology per end user (cost of web browser plug-ins)?
3. What kind of cost is associated with new network technology at the desktop? (Are the employees currently using a PC or a workstation; are they on a LAN or WAN?)
4. What is the cost of server hardware technology? (Do you have existing servers or will you need to buy new servers?)
5. What is the cost of server software?

6. What is the cost of development?
7. What are the estimated savings per year?

Quick calculation

$$((3+4+5+6)/1)+(1\times2)= \text{ cost per employee}$$
$$(7/1)\times3 = \text{ savings per employee}$$

If the cost per employee is less than or equal to the savings per employee, this is a good project.

Example

A company of 500 employees located in thirty offices in eight states wants to create a human resources home page. One hundred of the employees are located in the company's headquarters.

Existing Infrastructure:
Currently all the employees are in a client-server environment. Employees have PCs at their desk attached through Ethernet to UNIX servers. Local servers are attached to each other using a 100Mb Ethernet backbone. Remote offices fall into two classifications, depending on how many people are at the remote site. Class A sites have more than ten people and have T1 lines; class B sites have less than ten people and access HQ using switched 56. Employees on the road can call in to HQ using a 28.8 integrated modem in their PC.

Business Case:
Human resources sends a mailing to each employee every month that consists of an updated phone listing, a training schedule, and status on benefits. Quarterly, human resources sends out a detailed benefits program catalog, a 401k information sheet, and an updated training catalog. The monthly mailing costs $5 per employee, and the quarterly mailing costs $15 per employee. Shipping costs are $30 per office for the monthly mailing and $45 per office for the quarterly mailing. Yearly this program costs:

Current Costs:
Monthly cost = $2,500 (material) + $900 (mailing)
= $3,400 (monthly costs) × 8 (months) = $27,200

Figure 3-3. Example of Site Layout

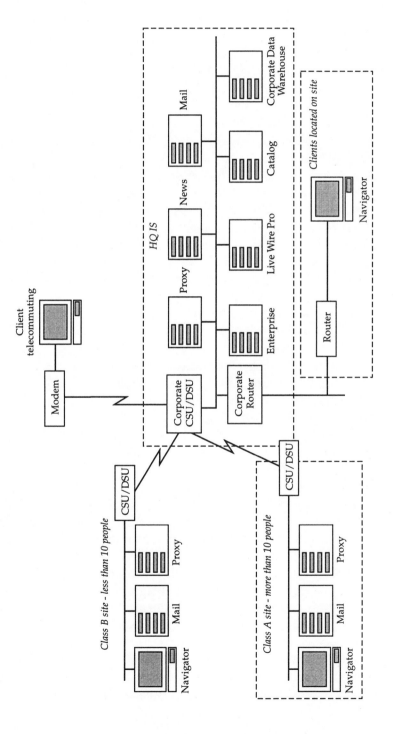

Quarterly cost = $7,500 (material) + $1,350 (mailing)
= $8,850 (quarterly) × 4 quarters = $35,400
Yearly cost = $62,600
Three-year cost = $187,800

Cost for Technology:
There is no hardware cost, since employees can use existing PCs, networks, and servers. PC web browser is Netscape Navigator, which costs $49 each. Server software is Netscape Enterprise Server, which costs $995 each. The company has ten servers at headquarters, thirty in the field. All the field servers are also used for communicating back to headquarters; each will get a copy of the web server software. Only one headquarters server is used for communication; only that server will get web software. Human resources is not planning on increasing costs, since the information was already being developed.

Browser cost = $24,500
Server cost = $30,845
IS retraining cost = $25,000
Internal employee retraining program = $10,000
Artist to create company web template and icons = $4,500
Cost to write simple cgi applications to display employee
    listing = $10,000
Total cost = $104,450
Savings over three years = $83,350

Internal Infrastructure:
Next, look at the infrastructure created by this project. If the company's IS department consists of mainframe JCL programmers and this project needs Java programmers, this may cost more than anticipated, since the company's technical strength is not being leveraged. Likewise, if the support organization has a strong database background and this product needs data communications support people, this project may cost more than anticipated since support staff can't cover for one another. It's a good idea to reuse internal infrastructure. This allows employees to migrate easily between projects, supporting growth and covering problems. Understand from the beginning if you are changing the way IS works. You can use this exercise as a means

of migrating people within the company to new skill sets. A good idea if you are planning on growing an IS discipline is to identify people who show aptitude and want to learn new technologies.

Finally, the company should look at its ability to reuse known technology. When creating new technology it is wise to limit the number of unknowns. Creating new technology based on new technology can lead to disaster. Many companies have learned this the hard way. There are many stories of programmers designing applications based on a presentation they received from a vendor. The company designs the application with this new component in mind. When they start developing the application, they find out the tools they need are not available or stable. Before creating an Internet/intranet technology, surf the web and see if another company has developed an application that uses similar elements. If you find a web site that has solved a similar problem, e-mail the site's web master and ask him what technology he used.

Creating a Requirements Document

Once there is a clear idea of what is being proposed, you need to create a requirements document. This document is the fundamental building block of a good project. Without a thorough assessment of what you are attempting to create at concept time, the best-designed and -executed solution will not necessarily fill a client's needs. Homework up front creates definition and direction in the future.

The requirements document should include sections on the following eight topics:

1. Goal and web solution
2. Concept statement
3. Scope of project
4. Benefits
5. Client demographics
6. Current client requirements

7. Future client requirements
8. Support requirements

How to Identify What Internal Procedures Can Best Be Adapted to an Intranet

First, identify a resource that your company uses. Determine whether there is a more effective way to perform this function. This is the first step in building a business case. It is the beginning of creating a requirements document. Remember, if you are developing an intranet, your client is the employee; if you are building an Internet, your client is the person accessing your site. The following explains how to identify the questions that need to be asked and where to find the information in order to create a requirements document.

Scope of project. Identify what you plan on accomplishing with this project. Write down the project's goal. How intrusive will this project be? Will this change the way the company does business? How will it affect employees' daily life? What is the scope of this project within the scope of the company's goals?

Benefits of project. Identify how this project will benefit your company. The benefit statement you created for your company earlier should be used now.

Client demographics. Knowledge of a client's demographics is necessary in order to identify who will use this application and how they will use it. By creating a generic picture of the typical client, later steps will be easier to answer. The typical questions you need to answer are:

- How should this product be visually and verbally presented to the client?
- What level of on-line help should be available?
- What management tools are needed to support the client?
- What kinds of questions will the IS support organization need to be prepared to handle?
- How will you need to position this new application to targeted clients?
- What kind of training will be necessary?

All of the answers generated from this information are instrumental in creating an effective product and an accurate budget.

The first step in identifying the client's demographics is to identify who the client is. Understanding the demographics identifies what the application and documentation should look and feel like. Answering no to a question does not mean an Internet/intranet project should not be attempted. Internet technology is geared for the less sophisticated computer person. The Internet's high use of graphics lends itself well to the less sophisticated user. An example of some questions that need to be answered regarding client demographics are:

- Are they sophisticated computer users?
- How educated is the least educated person who will be using this technology?
- Are the clients receptive to new ways of doing things?
- What language are the clients comfortable working with (English, French, Spanish)?

A finance plug-in to support cost accounting for a large multinational company will look physically different from an application that will support a manufacturing job shop. Accountants will be more receptive to reading and want to have backup documentation, whereas an application designed for a manufacturing floor should contain simple graphics. The same thought process should be used with plug-ins. An office environment with cubes will not be the right environment in which to run plug-in movies with sound or use speech recognition, while a movie plug-in explaining the proper installation of machine parts might be helpful for a manufacturing floor, or a voice recognition plug-in for a warehouse where a driver can verbally state his name, the name of his company, and the load being delivered and have this information displayed on the warehouse screen to save time.

Current client requirements. It is important to understand why and how clients are currently performing the task you plan on automating with an Internet/intranet application, as well as what changes clients would like to see. Many people feel comfortable with the applications they are currently using even if these applications are cumbersome and inefficient. People feel safe with an application. They don't feel comfortable with change. If the way they are currently working is to be changed, it is necessary to understand how this change will affect the client. If you find out there are utilities/words/formats they like, you can create the new program to mimic these things. It is necessary to identify and predict the client reaction. Decisions can be made based on an understanding that the change will hurt or help the acceptance of the product. If clients are familiar with using a certain sheet of paper, you can design the screen to look like this paper. If a current application uses menus, you can create the new application with menus and icons. You can take the approach that you will facilitate change instead of inflict change. If you are creating an intranet and you find resistance (fear) when talking to user groups, you should budget in small-group training. This is one way to successfully initiate resistant clients to new technology. Choose people sympathetic to the client to perform the training. If you are hiring new people or consultants to do the training, choose people who meet the demographics or work well with the demographics of the groups you are training. The groups being trained will feel more comfortable with people similar to themselves. For example, if your application is for a manufacturing environment and most of your manufacturing workers speak Spanish, you would want to choose someone who feels comfortable explaining how to use the utilities in Spanish.

Many times IS departments overlook talking to the clients. They believe that they know their fellow employees or customers and that they have enough client information. Companies have developed applications thinking that employees or customers were using the product for one reason, while the employees or customers were actually using the application for an entirely different reason. If you don't talk to your client, basic needs may be overlooked and positive features may be designed out. Additionally, if you decide there is a better way to solve a problem but when you interview clients you feel they are comfortable with the current solution or you feel clients are resistant to change, you can involve a client representative in your team.

The client representative can give you feedback. You can use this feedback when designing the application or client training.

Approaching clients. It is necessary to talk directly to clients to get accurate information. Talking to functional managers is another step in creating a requirements document. Don't short-cut the process. Take the time to talk directly with the clients who will be using the system. They will make or break acceptance of this new technology. The easiest but least effective way to talk to clients is through a questionnaire sent to them. Avoid this method, since the information tends to be inaccurate, as there is no control over who actually fills out or sends in the questionnaire. Questionnaires by mail are good for periodic surveys, but for new product development spend the extra time to get good, accurate feedback. A much better and more accurate way to get client information is to talk to the clients directly by phone or to visit them. Most clients are flattered to be asked their opinion. By going to the source, you get timely, accurate information.

Designing a survey. The first step in an accurate survey is to design a client questionnaire. When designing a questionnaire, decide what questions you want answered. Write down all the things you think you might want to know. Prioritize those questions. Typically you won't have time to ask more than ten questions. Design survey questions that will provide you with experiential information. This is harder to do and harder to analyze than a direct question, but the information received will be more accurate. Trial lawyers don't ask prospective jury members if they are prejudiced. They ask them what experiences they have had with a particular group, or they ask them what they have heard about a particular group. Experiential questions give better information. For example, since you will now be using a graphical user interface (GUI), don't ask clients if they like GUIs. Ask them if they ever used a product that had a GUI. If they say yes, ask them how they liked using that GUI. What was it about that GUI they liked? Why was this better than other GUIs? A note about icons used in GUIs: Icons are like art; everyone has an opinion and no one ever agrees. Never ask clients if they like the look of an icon. Ask an experiential question. Ask them if they like identifying information by clicking on an icon or clicking on text. If they tell you they don't know the name of an application, they just know they need to click on that "funny green design," you know the icon has been successful. People don't have to like or understand a design; the design is successful if it is easily recognized. By asking experiential questions, you find out how the client feels, not how they think they should feel. Experiential questions provide a better picture of how clients will react when they get this new application. The information received now can be successfully used later when you present your business case to management. The goal of this survey is to find out the level of comfort potential clients might have with a GUI application. If you need additional detail, remember to ask the clients why when they give you a one-word yes or no answer. Client information gives you good feedback and direction when designing, developing, and marketing your application. Client information is the basis for decisions throughout the process.

Sample Questionnaire

- Have you ever used a computer that allows you to make a selection by touching a picture (web browser, existing application, tourist computer at train stations, bridal registry at a department store)?
- Did you feel comfortable using that computer?
- Did pictures help you choose your selection?
- Did you find it easy to find what you wanted by navigating through a picture-oriented program?

Sample Survey for HR Business Case

- Do you receive the HR monthly mailing?
- Do you have a copy on your desk? Where is it? What is the date? (This is a good way to have an idea how it is being used, how current.)
- Do you ever misplace the information when you need it most?
- What do you do when you misplace it?
- Would you feel comfortable accessing the information if it were in a word-processing document on your PC? (If they

like it on their computer, they will like it just as much if it is on a web site.)

- How often do you look up information and find that the sheet is not current?
- How often do you use this information?

Filling in the survey. Now that a survey has been created, try it out on someone who matches the client's demographics. Fine-tune the questionnaire to make sure the objectives will be met. Take a sample of ten to fifteen clients and call them. If they provide similar answers, you probably have a good idea of their needs. If the answers seem skewed, call ten more clients. Ten to fifty clients should be all that are needed, depending on how broadly used the product is. Remember, clients in different locations may view information differently. Europeans might enjoy on-line information more than domestic clients, since Europe does not have easy access to headquarters. Don't prejudice the people you are calling. If you give them lots of background information and lead them to the answer you want, you will get skewed information. It might meet your needs now, but it will lead to an unsuccessful project. Your goal during this phase is to find out what your client likes.

Focus group. A next step to get good client information is to create focus groups. Ask five to ten clients to attend a round-table meeting. A round table or focus group is just that; a room with a round-table where you can bring in a targeted group of people, ask them questions, and monitor their responses. For the round table, create a set of experiential questions similar to those you created for the phone. Round tables are interesting since clients may give different answers on the phone from in person and in a group. This extra step is important, since decisions are not always made by one person. Since the application is using Internet technology, find a few companies who solve similar problems with Internet solutions. Show this to the people in the round table; let them try using the Internet application. Then ask them your questions. Make the round table, questions, and Internet demonstrations simple and informal. People are more candid when they feel they are among friends. Write down any good sound bites that come from people at the round table.

Sound bites work well when you are creating a presentation to sell your idea.

A word of warning: Don't bias the questionnaire. Don't give the people questioned any more information than they would receive if they were asked to evaluate the product without any access to an IS representative.

Future client requirements. Future Internet applicants can be created based on the information gathered. You can use this information as a stepping-stone to broaden client services, cut overhead costs, or increase client productivity. Your first application might be rolled out to a limited number of clients. Identify who else might be interested in the application you are creating. If you include future clients in the survey, you might save time in the long run. Future clients may have very different needs from existing clients. Don't overlook these differences.

Support organization. Don't forget to tap this resource. Support organizations like help desk or customer support continually answer client questions. Again, create a questionnaire designed for support people. Host a support organization round table. Some companies are afraid of asking internal people, since they are afraid a round table will turn into a gripe session. A session, properly managed, with a set agenda and clear goals, will be informative and positive. For an existing product the support organization should have created a "wish list." This is a list made up of client requests. A wish list is an excellent foundation for the feature/functionality list.

Effect on Infrastructure

After you figure out the scope of the project, you should meet with the people in your IS organization who are responsible for laying out, managing, and supporting applications that run on your servers. Discuss the implications of adding these new applications to your environment. The infrastructure folks will need time to draw up a preliminary plan outlining how this will affect the current environment. You will need to get a general estimate on how much it will cost the company to add servers to support Internet/intranet applications.

Using the Internet

Companies who sell Internet products are a wealth of knowledge on Internet applications. Netscape, Microsoft, and IBM (Lotus) all have nicely articulated customer stories and sample applications. Surf the Internet, and spend some time reviewing these stories; they can be great references when creating your business case.

Creating the Feature/Functionality Report

Once the information has been obtained for the requirement document, a feature/functionality document can be created. A feature/functionality document takes each feature that was recommended or identified in any of the steps defined in the client requirements document, and lists it. You can then take this feature/functionality list and the concept document described earlier in the chapter and write an overview explaining what the product should look like. The feature/functionality list should be prioritized by company direction. The prioritized list needs to have at least three sections: *A*, *B*, and *C*. *A* lists the features that must be in the product for the product to work; *B* lists the features that would be good to have; *C* lists the features that would make the project exciting or special. A workable feature list document has now been created.

Report Review

You should review this document with other technologists. You can create an estimate for each feature based on how long you believe it will take to develop that feature. You need to annotate what development processes can be shortened by putting more people on the feature and what development cycles are "pregnant." You can't get three women pregnant and get a baby in three months. There are some development cycles that will take three person-months if you have three, six, or nine developers associated with it. By understanding the pregnant development

Table 3-2. Sample Feature/Functionality Report

Item	Rank	Dev. Time	Pregnant Process
Icon to access program	A	2 days	Yes
Design process	A	5 days	Yes
Put in partial name and see all occurrences	A	3 days	
Scroll down to names by entering first letter of first name or last name	B	2 days	
Ability to view list by first name, last name, department, or location	B	2 days	
Screen format to look like current paper format	A	3 days	
Include conference rooms	B	1 day	
Optionally view employee name, e-mail, fax, phone, address, department	B	1 day	
Double click location, view building, layout—where person sits	C	2 weeks	
Include picture of employee	C	1 week	
Double click e-mail—shoots you into e-mail with person's name in "send to" location and your name in "from" location	C	1 week	
Easy-print interface; customized information prints out looking nice	A	1 week	

cycles, you can more easily flag areas that cannot be shortened and highlight areas where potential slips might occur.

Cost for Development

By creating this basic overview, IS should be able to estimate the cost of developing an application or web site. The following is a sample of items that should be estimated. Your list might be simpler or have more detail. Don't make this matrix too complex. Overestimate your expenses; there are always those things that get overlooked or processes that take longer than expected. The information in this matrix will be used for the cost estimate in your business's plan. After you get business plan approval you can create a detailed design where you can develop a more accurate cost.

Table 3-3. Cost Matrix

Item	Existing/ Upgrade	New/ Vendor	Estimated Cost
ISP			
Internal web master			
Internal server layout			
Existing phone/T1 lines			
Web software			
Client software			
Home page design			
Web site layout design/development			
Application design/development			

Staffing

The largest cost for any project is usually the human cost. It's important to identify from the start what type of site you are planning on creating. If you want a simple passive site that is primarily for Internet presence with static information, you will not need to plan for a lot of people. If your plan is to have a dynamic site that will be a web destination, you will need to hire a team of people to run your site. For instance, if you are a realtor and you are planning on putting all your house listings up on the Internet, you might want to provide on-line walking tours that include local maps showing the house's location and nearby facilities, house layout, and features. You will probably need to hire or contract professional staff to run your site if you plan on keeping your listings current. If you are a housing developer who has developed a new housing project that you plan on selling over a two-year period, you probably can have one site created and modify it periodically.

Web Master

If you run your own Internet/intranet site, you will need to hire a web master. The web master is responsible for making sure your site is live and functioning. The ideal web master has a strong UNIX systems administration background and is very familiar with configuring and running TCP/IP networks. The person should be comfortable writing C and script programs. An experienced UNIX administrator will have little problem learning html, CGI, and learning how to manage web server applications. There are a lot of IS people out there with this kind of background. Good web masters do not come cheap. Another solution is to hire an independent company or individual to provide your web management. There are many local ISPs (Internet service providers). ISPs have teams of web masters that for a fee can provide you with any service you need. If you are starting your first web site, the best solution is to go with an ISP. It will be much easier to justify bringing the web management in-house as your site's services grow. The primary reasons for bringing Internet web management inside are control and cost. By definition an intranet is an inside server. An IS organization should view an intranet as another UNIX application server and hire accordingly. The intranet web master will need the same UNIX, TCP/IP skill set as an Internet web master. The intranet web master's focus will be on optimizing the company's internal infrastructure and providing timely access to clients.

Web Editor

The web editor is responsible for managing content on your site, including page placement, web flow, page content, and visuals. If you have a basic passive site with relatively static information, you probably won't need a web editor. If you have an active site with dynamic information, most likely you will need to hire a company to act as your web editor or hire a web editor. Highly dynamic sites should be viewed like a magazine or newspaper. How often will you pick up the same magazine? Do you want your site to be viewed as an encyclopedia—a place to go for reference information? Or a newspaper—a destination people continually sign on to in order to find the latest information? Once you make a decision identifying what kind of site you want to have you will know if you need to hire a web editor. There is a good chance that if you hire an editor you will need to hire a web site team. The team will consist of writers and designers. A team may consist of the following types of people: writers for web content, artists for web design elements, QA to test the site, and traffic to manage web content publishing. A dynamic web site is like a magazine. The web editor and design team most likely will report to your marketing organization. Their focus will be on selling your company and products to clients.

Table 3-4. Decision Matrix

	Passive Site	*Active Site*
Static Site Changes infrequently—should not need a web editor	On-line brochures	On-line schedule checking, downloads
Dynamic Changes frequently—destination location—will need a web editor	On-line magazine	Changing copy, interactive applications

An intranet web site will also need flow coordination. The difference is that an intranet web editor will report through IS. He will be less interested in web content and presentation and more interested in flow coordination and application integration. For an intranet web editor find a person with good project management skills. Expect that a web editor will lead a team of people responsible for managing the site.

Design Team

Your Internet web site is your virtual company. First impressions count. Don't get cheap on the site design. It is always important to provide a professional face to clients. There are lots of inexpensive tools to create web sites. Use these tools to update content. Hire a professional to design your site. It will make the difference. First impressions are not as important for an intranet. It is still worthwhile to have a design team create a few basic templates.

By this time you have identified a potential application that can benefit from Internet technology, performed a quick check to see if it is a good financial business case, identified how this will affect your internal infrastructure and what additional people will be needed to support the site or applications, called potential clients and gotten some feedback, and created a list of features and annotated a time frame to develop each feature.

A word of warning: Don't get greedy. Solve one thing with an Intranet/intranet business case. It will take a lot of time and energy to get all the clients up on a browser and to get your servers to be functional web sites. The first application will be a test application. Don't choose a mission-critical application; don't choose an overly fancy application. A home page that uses already created information that the creators need to publish is a good first application. Once the initial infrastructure is in place, clients can access the information, and IS has had some experience working a web site, you can ease yourself into more creative applications. If the first site is successful, client departments will want to see their department's information on the home page. Company demands will easily make an intranet grow.

4

Creating the Business Case

The role of a business case is to present an overview of the concept, solution, benefit, cost, and, if applicable, return for a project. Don't get too complicated when building the business case. Typically the people you are presenting to are decision makers. They will get lost in the details of a complicated business case. Present them with clear, high-level facts. Don't assume that what seems obvious to you is obvious to them. State the obvious; don't linger on it. Detail the benefits of your business case. Keep the actual presentation short and to the point. If you need details, bring your requirements document and feature/functionality report for reference. Depending on how your company works, you probably have not yet developed or designed your system. To head off detailed design questions, make a point of stating the objective of the presentation. The goal of the concept presentation is to get corporate funding and approval to perform the next phase in creating an Internet/intranet. The next phase (Chapter 5) is where you will perform a detailed design.

Laying Out the Presentation

There are a few key points you will need to highlight when presenting your business case:

Goal of the presentation. Make sure you clearly articulate what you are doing and what you want from your audience. For example, you might want to say: "This presentation is to provide you with a concept of the direction we would like to proceed in. If you approve this concept we will perform a detailed study."

Goal of the project. In Chapter 3 we created one simple, easily articulated goal. This goal will be the central idea throughout the life of the project. Having a clear, unchanging goal keeps a project focused. Before deciding on your goal and making your presentation to the executive staff, clearly understand the company's goals. If executives are not interested in solving the problem you identified, the best idea will not get approval. Find out the decision makers' "hot button" and provide a goal and benefit that solve their biggest problems. Later you can solve problems that executive staff might not understand are problems. This is referred to as a *resulting solution.*

Benefit of the project. Benefits go hand in hand with goals. Don't overlook providing a benefits statement. Many people think benefits are apparent. A benefit might be obvious to you, but it might not be to the person to whom you are presenting. Make sure you are sympathetic to the listener. You don't want the listener to walk away with the wrong impression. The listener might think a solution solves one problem while you are planning a site that actually solves (benefit) a different problem. Another good reason for clearly stating the benefit up front is that it saves the listener the energy of figuring out the benefit. If the listeners are figuring out the benefit, they are not listening to you. It's hard enough keeping listeners focused on what you're saying when presenting; don't create situations that can lose a listener. The goal of most Internet applications is to increase information to customers, expand customer base, increase services to customers, increase company recognition, or provide an additional distribution channel. The benefit is to increase customer satisfaction, decrease internal resources, or increase market share and revenue. The bottom line is that an Internet application should decrease costs or increase revenue. The benefit of most intranet applications is to increase communications, provide education, or decrease the cost of the way business is currently done. The bottom-line benefit of an intranet is to increase productivity or decrease costs.

Table 4-1. Internet Goal-Benefit Matrix

Goal	Benefit
Create a new source for sales leads	Increase sales, increase revenue
Provide an additional distribution channel	Increase sales, increase market share
Provide company or product information to established customers	Increase customer satisfaction
Establish a clearly identified image	Differentiate yourself in your industry
Off-load current telephone support organizations by supporting clients over the Internet	Increase support while decreasing internal expense
Provide an international presence	Explore new markets
Provide additional services to existing customers	Increase service, differentiate yourself, increase customer service
More timely response to sales leads	Increase customer satisfaction

Clearly Identify Why Using Internet/Intranet Technology Will Result in This Goal

It is a good idea to provide an overview of how the goal and benefit will actually work. Many times the listener at your presentation is not familiar with the details of using an Internet. Give them enough information so they feel comfortable. For example:

■ *Create a new source for sales leads.* Our company can have a home site on the Internet. Through joint relationships (pointers) and strategically positioned banners, we can advertise our location to potential customers. Potential customers can visit our site, obtain information on our product, and be directed to locations where they can purchase our product.

Table 4-2. Intranet Goal-Benefit Matrix

Goal	Benefit
Use the technology to cut costs on a current project	Effective use of budget (save money, provide same services with a smaller budget, or create expanded services with the same budget)
Provide same-day worldwide corporate information access	Increased communication should increase productivity, get more things done with the same budget
Infrastructure to upgrade existing systems with new features	New features should increase employee productivity
Provide corporate-wide collaboration services	Increase employee productivity
Provide on-line training	Save money by providing training at the desk. Increase productivity by providing instantaneous training from the client point of view.

- *Provide an additional distribution channel.* Our company can create a home site and display our products at this site. Customers can view the product and ask questions on our chat line. Customers wanting to purchase products can choose products and enter in their credit card number. This will generate an order that will result in a product being shipped to the customer.

- *Provide company or product information to established customers.* Existing customers will be provided a URL location. They then have instantaneous access to the latest information on company policies and products. This will increase customer knowledge and satisfaction at little cost to the company.

- *Establish a clearly identified image.* Our company will have the same access to Internet customers as our much larger competition does. A clear, professional web site provides an image larger and richer than we actually are.

- *More timely response to sales leads.* Infrastructure can be created to automatically respond to customers or automatically tag salespeople with customer questions.

Effect of the Internet/Intranet on Your Company

Provide information on what you visualize the effect of the Internet or intranet will be on your company's people and IS infrastructure. Depending on how big a site is and how intrusive your plan is, an Internet/intranet site might have little effect or a lot of effect on employees' daily life. Make it clear up front how this new technology will affect work groups. If your company just wants to have an information site for customers, employees might not have any access to the Internet and will not be affected by this technology. For an intranet, executives might be concerned that putting a web browser on everyone's desk might create a company of web surfers. State the amount of intrusion and overcome common objections before they are brought up. For example, you might want to tell executives that all employees will have a web browser on their desk. This web browser will be an employee's window (GUI) to the intranet applications. All employees will have an Internet e-mail address, but only employees with approval will have access to the WWW. Specifically tell the listener that access to the WWW can be controlled.

Cost of the Solution

Before presenting, you should have figured out an initial cost. Make sure you pad your cost estimate. Everything always costs more than you initially think; it's easy to forget something. As the axiom goes, "You can only go to the well once." Set management's level of expectation correctly concerning the cost of the project. You don't want to get caught underestimating your project and having to go back to management asking for more money.

Time Frame

You should have a draft of a time line if you completed the steps in Chapter 3. Present this time line.

ROI or Margin

If applicable, present an ROI (return on investment) or Margin analysis. An ROI tells the company how much money it is making from a project based on total cost of developing and manufacturing. The margin tells a company how much money it is making from a project based on the cost of manufacturing. The ROI and margin analyses are financial indicators identifying the percentage return that will be received by investing money in a project. An ROI is calculated by dividing the cost of a project by the expected profit. A margin calculation is based on price and cost of a project. When building your business case, check with your finance officer to find out the return your company looks for from a project. Find out from your CFO what your company uses to figure out financial viability of a project.

ROI/Margin Example:

- An application was developed for $50,000.
- It will cost $20 (printing and mailing) to send out a manual to each customer explaining how to use the application.
- There are 10,000 customers.
- The application will save the company $100 per customer (price or savings per customer).
- The company should have a $1,000,000 savings (or revenue).

ROI = 15%

Revenue/development cost; $1,000,000/$50,000 = 20%

Margin = 80%

(Price − cost)/price; 100–20/100 = 80%

How to Begin

Detach yourself from your company. Take the time to write a simple business case similar to those written below. Too often people get caught in the details. Detaching yourself gives you the ability to view a situation from many angles. This lets you prove the best solution and present an easy-to-follow business case. However, make sure you answer each of the questions outlined at the beginning of this chapter.

You now should have the basis for creating a business case presentation. Break the presentation down to logical thoughts. The rule of thumb is not to put more than five bullets on a page. Keep the ideas simple. Keep the presentation simple. Use pictures only if they assist you in illustrating a point. Unless you are really good at telling jokes, don't! It will make you look foolish. Giving a presentation is like telling a story. Make sure your presentation flows. Don't get caught up in detail. Your goal is to sell your idea; don't lose the listener. You should be driving the listeners to come to the decision you want them to make.

Outlined below are basic business cases for six different types of companies that have very different needs. You should build a similar model for your business case.

Scenario 1—A Simple Internet Web Site

Developing the Business Case

- *Background.* Company that sells, installs, and monitors home and business alarms.
- *Customer demographics.* The customer base is 75% residential, 25% commercial. Estimated value of house prices with belongings ranges from $150,000 to over $1,000,000. The latest customer survey found that over 80% of their residential customers have a home computer while 100% of their commercial customers have a computer. They do not know what percentage of their customers have Internet access.
- *Web goal.* To maintain an image of being on the forefront of technology, to provide additional channels to advertise their products and services, and to provide a source for existing customers to review additional products they can add to their current installation.
- *Competition.* They are competing with a large multinational company that has a division that sells home and busi-

ness alarms and a local company around their size. The company their size is a conservative company that innovates slowly. The alarm company's current strategy for differentiation is to present themselves as a local company that understands and cares about the well-being of the community while being a technological leader in securing customers' property.

- *Budget.* The company has not budgeted for a web site. Most of the money the company currently spends for marketing is on new brochure designs. Advertising is primarily through radio and billboards. The marketing manager, who's championing this project, believes she can go to the president and ask for the additional funds.

- *Company IS infrastructure.* The company has a classic three-tier client server architecture. The IS manager has been following the recent explosion of Internet technology offerings but has been reluctant to push the company in that direction. The company is very conservative when it comes to computer access. A security breach would quickly make its way into the local news, providing bad press.

- *Solution.* The IS manager contacted a local ISP. The ISP will provide the alarm company with their own name server. The marketing manager will head up the project for content and response. Recently the company rewrote and redesigned their brochures. The new brochure pack includes a nicely designed company profile, an explanation of services, illustration of services, and an explanation of response services. Marketing has designed an internal bulletin for sales, highlighting the most frequently asked questions (FAQs). The company has a number of documents that customers need to fill in. Customers typically are faxed these documents. The company wants to provide clients with documents that can be downloaded and printed at the client's site. The advertising agency that designed the brochures is working with a company that designs web pages. The web design company quoted the alarm company $5,000 to lay out the web site, reformat existing brochures, create links to appropriate sites, create banner templates, create mascot images, create downloadable documents, and create a FAQs html web document format.

▪ *Security.* Since the Internet web site resides on the server of the ISP, there are no security implications for the alarm company. The alarm company calls up the ISP to upload and download e-mail and to publish new information.

▪ *Infrastructure.* The IS manager will buy a modem and an outside line for the marketing manager. The marketing manager is planning on taking a one-day class that explains marketing and publishing on the web. She will use Netscape Navigator Gold for publishing and for e-mail. The IS manager set up and configured her PC/modem and software.

Cost for Internet Web Access

- $5,000 for web content
- $500 for class on web publishing
- $150 for new modem for marketing manager
- $79 for Netscape Navigator Gold
- $30 a month ($360 a year) for name server ISP access
- Total cost for year one = $6,089
- Total cost for three years = $6,809 (average cost for each of three years = $2,270 over three years)

Note: The business case for this type of web site should be focused on the low-cost entry to a potential channel for prospecting and supporting customers. There is not enough good data available to attempt to build a business case based on potential revenue.

Follow-Up

The advertising agency has provided the company with the html files for all the brochures turned into web pages. The marketing manager can change text and republish pages if content or prices change. All questions are sent to an e-mail "info" name into which the marketing manager can dial and download the e-mail daily. The company plans on monitoring this passive site. The company has included their WWW

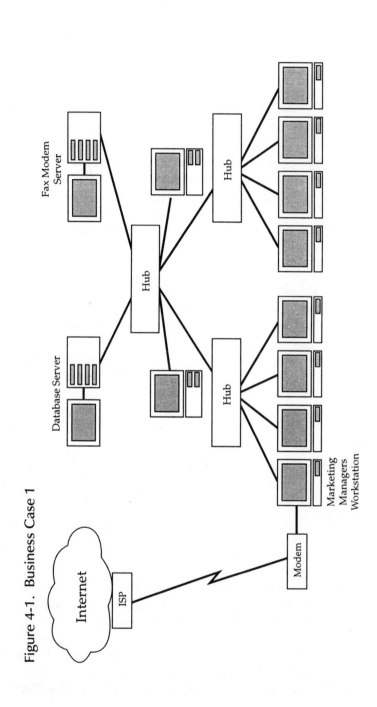

Figure 4-1. Business Case 1

site address on all their advertising. If they find they are getting favorable responses, they would like to add a chat section to their WWW page. The marketing manager is writing down how much time she spends answering e-mails. She is categorizing the e-mail she receives so she can identify where the calls would come in normally (sales, customer support). From this information she can put together a cost justification for additional resources or move support to the appropriate group. She hopes this site will create enough interest so that she can hire a person responsible for managing the site. She is also reviewing what additional features they can add to the site to pull in more qualified potential customers.

Business Case Presentation

Alarm Company
Creating a Company Presence on the Internet

Benefits

- Stated company goal is to provide the best service to our customers.
- A web site will provide twenty-four-hour/seven-day-a-week information.
- Instant answers to frequently asked questions.
- Instant access to the most requested faxes.

Why the Internet

- Hot new technology meets our image as a hot technology company.
- Web "surfer" demographics include our targeted customers.
- Low-cost, high-impact opportunity to present our products.
- Opportunity to test a potential new sales and marketing support channel.
- Easy, low-cost entry.

Web Site Goal

- Maintain an image of being on the forefront of technology.
- Present company's offerings to a wider market.
- Provide a depository of information for existing and potential customers.
- Differentiate us from the competition.

Web Site Content

- Passive web site.
- Reformat current brochures for web viewing.
- Provide area for customers to read about new services.
- Provide area for customers to view FAQs.
- Provide downloads of often-requested documents.
- Provide e-mail access for customers and prospects to
    1. Find out more about the company or our offerings.
    2. Schedule an on-site sales call.
    3. Ask a question.

Effect on Company

- Initially no new people or equipment.
- Will not change the way we currently do business.
- Web site will not be disruptive of daily business.
- Employees will not have web or e-mail access.

Cost for Internet Web Access

- $5,000 for web content (design)
- $500 for class on web publishing
- $150 for new modem for marketing manager
- $79 for Netscape Navigator Gold
- $30 a month ($360 a year) for name server ISP access
- Total cost for year one = $6,089
- Total cost for three years = $6,909 (average cost = $2,303 over three years)

Recommendation

- Marketing department responsible for creating and managing the web site.
- Advertise WWW address in brochures, print, and radio.
- Maintain log of
  1. Number of hits.
  2. Types of inquiries.
- Report back, after the site is live for six months, on findings.

Time Line

- Design firm can turn out current brochures into web content in four weeks.
- Estimated time to go live: six weeks.

Executive Action

- Approval of project
- Approval of budget

Scenario 2 —Internet Access

Developing the Business Case

- *Background.* Sixty-six person law firm, consists of thirty lawyers, three paralegal, three support staff, thirty secretaries.

- *Employee demographics.* All employees have a PC on their desk. All employees are comfortable using WordPerfect and the time/billing system. Lawyers are responsible for their own research.

- *Goal.* The law firm is one of twenty-five law firms representing a large company in a very complex lawsuit. The senior partners of the twenty-five law firms have been discussing ways the firms can access each other's large and growing archive of legal documents pertaining to this case. None of the law firms want to give up control of their documents. Additionally lawyers have been pushing to work at home on cases while receiving access to the company's document server and time/billing system. The lawyers have also found that a few universities have put sections of their law library on-line. Lawyers are asking for Internet access to do research.

▪ *Action*. The partner responsible for the law firm's infrastructure calls the company that manages their IS infrastructure. The following three applications are outlined: (1) Password-protected Internet access to client case file, (2) intranet access to company files, (3) Internet access to the WWW. The lawyer highlights that the law firm is concerned about illegal access and has not budgeted for this.

▪ *Law firm's IS infrastructure*. The law firm has a simple two-tier client-server architecture. All sixty-six PCs connect into a large server via Ethernet and Novell Netware. The server is the depository for the law firm's WordPerfect documents and the time/billing system. Each PC runs the client version of the time/billing system and has WordPerfect.

▪ *Solution*. Everyone in the firm will get a copy of Netscape Navigator. The law firm will add an NT PC (NT is Microsoft's multi-user operating system) that will communicate with the current Novell server using fast Ethernet. The NT PC will have Novell's Site Builder software and an ISDN line (ISDN is a phone service that supports two 64kb lines).

▪ *Security*. The ISP provides fire wall protection; additionally the only access to their server will be through password protection. There will be three levels of security access. Level one access will be the simplest. This password protection will be given to the twenty-four other law offices, allowing them access to only the files on the large account. Level two will be for the firm's lawyers so they can access the time/billing system and law firm archive. Level three has complete access to everything.

Cost for Solution

▪ $5,000 for PC with Novell Site Builder
▪ $1,000 for IS outsource company to install and optimize new technology, set up password-protected sections

- $300 for ISDN card
- $30 a month ($360 a year) for name server ISP access
- $49 each for Navigator (sixty-six PCs = $3,234)
- Total cost for year one = $9,894
- Total cost for three years = $10,614 (average cost = $3,538 over three years)

Follow-Up

The law firm has found out that an added benefit of this solution is that since they have an Internet name server, they now have Internet e-mail access. The law firm has decided to move interoffice mail from paper to e-mail. Lawyers telecommuting can now check messages. The other twenty-four law firms agreed to add a similar configuration to their office. Lawyers working on the same case with another law firm can now send e-mail messages to each other, saving time, facilitating communications, and creating an automatic message log. The law firm is looking into increasing services by creating a news chat group for shared cases. That way lawyers can input comments on a case. The next lawyer to review the case not only gets the case's documents, but a running history of the lawyers' comments.

Business Case Presentation

Law Firm
Using Internet Technologies to Access Legal Records

Goal and Benefit

- Increase information flow.
- Save time and money by providing infrastructure to access information directly.

Situation

- Need to provide controlled access of case records to other law firms.

Figure 4-2. Business Case 2

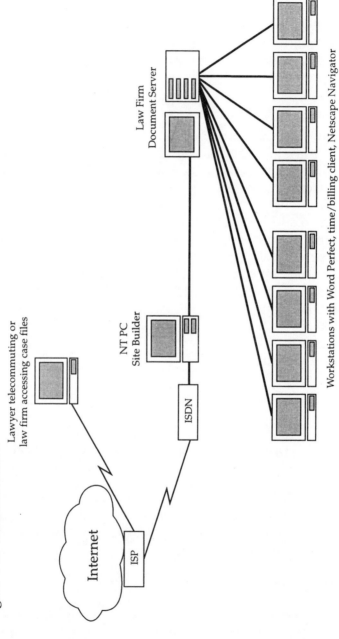

Lawyer telecommuting or
law firm accessing case files

Internet

ISP

ISDN

NT PC
Site Builder

Law Firm
Document Server

Workstations with Word Perfect, time/billing client, Netscape Navigator

- Want to provide telecommuting infrastructure.
- Want to provide access to WWW databases.

Why the Internet

- Easy, low-cost entry
- Little overhead needed to synch up other law offices
- Low-risk solution
  —Web site is not published
  —Only access is through password-protected screens
- Expandable for the future
  —E-mail
  —Internet advertising

Effect on the Law Firm

- No new people are needed.
- Employees can use the systems they are currently using.
- Provides employees with the latest technology.

Cost for Internet Web Access

- $5,000 for PC with Novell Site Builder
- $1,000 for IS to hire contractors to install and optimize new technology, create password protection layers
- $300 for ISDN card
- $30 a month ($360 a year) for name server ISP access
- $49 each for Navigator (sixty-six PCs = $3,234)
- Total cost for year one = $9,894
- Total cost for three years = $10,614 (average cost = $3,538 over three years)

Time Line/Action

- Need two weeks to get site builder computer installed.
- Internet access takes twenty-four hours.
- Partner needs to "sell" solution to other law firms.

Scenario 3—Internet

Developing the Business Case

- *Background.* A large manufacturer was planning on creating an application that would allow distributors to have the ability to order new supplies through the application. The company has over 600 distributors located in twenty-seven countries.

- *Customer demographics.* The company polled the distributor purchasing agents and found out that all purchasing agents had a PC or equivalent computer on their desk. About ten percent of the customers currently have access to an outside line, an e-mail address, or access to the Internet. Based on what purchasing agents said, the number of agents with Internet access should double in the next twelve months.

- *Goal.* Currently customers need to fax a form to the company's sales offices to place an order. The salesperson then reviews all orders, signs off on the order after checking the company's credit history, and gives the order to an administrator to enter into the system. The company believes that by automating this process it can speed up order flow, simplify ordering procedures, and cut down on unnecessary paperwork. IS studied this problem and found out that a typical order takes five days to get into the system and takes one man-hour of processing. The company processes over 1,000 orders a week. Marketing has agreed to turn the company's data sheets and newsletters into web content. Marketing communications is heading up a project to make the site informative and attractive.

- *Action.* IS has been reading about the benefit of Internet applications. They believe that an Internet application can solve the problem. They were looking for a noninvasive solution. In the past they attempted to solve this problem but found that there was no one simple solution that worked across product lines and could be used in all twenty-seven countries.

- *IS infrastructure.* The company has a classic client-server model with PCs on employees' desks, UNIX and NT file servers, and mainframes running Oracle as their large data warehouse transaction-processing machines. They have a small, sharp team of communication professionals that run their SNA (IBM's protocol), Ethernet network. Three years ago the company decided to make TCP/IP the standard networking protocol and has been migrating toward this goal. They have two open positions in the IS communications department. One of their existing IS people is an experienced UNIX and TCP/IP systems administrator.

- *Solution.* The company plans on creating a CGI application using Internet technology. They will create their own web site. The existing UNIX systems administrator will go to a training class on web mastering; his systems administrator position will eventually be filled by one of the open positions. They will add two router/fire walls and place a web server, mail server, and proxy wall outside of the corporate fire wall. They decided to go with the extra layer of fire wall protection to overcome company privacy concerns. So that the company does not create a workforce of web surfers, employees will need management approval to access web sites outside the intranet. Customers can continue faxing orders into the sales office. By using a standard Internet web browser, customers will have the option of ordering by accessing the Internet site. Once on the Internet site, customers can view the latest information on current products or choose the icon for placing the order. When they choose the icon option, they are asked to input their customer number (this number works as a password). The CGI application will automatically confirm that the customer number is good and that the distributor is approved to order products. The screen for entering an order looks just like the paper form the purchasing agent has been use to using. After the order is placed, the customer will be asked to confirm his shipping address, and a schedule of the ship date will be displayed. The order will automatically generate an internal e-mail notifying the customer's salesperson about this new order and generating an e-mail to the distributor confirming the details of the order placed.

- *Security.* The company will purchase a PC for the fire wall. Additionally the CGI application will reside on the web server. The customer data will be behind the fire wall on the IBM mainframe.

- *Access.* One transaction can save the company $50. The company is looking at a program in which they will provide customers who order over $20,000 of product a year and don't have an Internet with a web browser, a modem, and Internet access free if they use the Internet to order products. The IS group will preconfigure the browser so it automatically opens on the company's home page.

Cost for Solution

- $5,000 for fire wall PC
- $35,000 for UNIX web server
- $4,000 for Netscape SuiteSpot
- $25,000 to write the CGI program
- $5,000 for CSU/DSU
- $1,000 a month, $12,000 a year for communications lines
- $10,000 for a year for art and content for the server home page
- $60,000 for training salespeople and customers about the new program
- Year one cost = $156,000
- Three-year cost = $200,000, average cost per year = $66,666

Expected Savings

- The company expects 10% of the customers will use the application the first year, 20% the second year, and 40% the third year.
- Cost per employee hour is averaged at $50.
- Savings
    Year one savings:
    —It takes an hour of employee time to process one order.
    —The average cost per employee is $50.
    —The company expects an average of 100 on-line transactions per week.
    —The expected savings per week should be $5,000.
    —The company is open 50 weeks a year.
    —The company expects a $250,000 savings in year one.

Year two savings:

—It takes an hour of employee time to process one order.

—The average cost per employee is $50.

—The company expects an average of 200 on-line transactions per week.

—The expected savings per week should be $10,000.

—The company is open 50 weeks a year.

—The company expects a $500,000 savings in year two.

Year three savings:

—It takes an hour of employee time to process one order.

—The average cost per employee is $50.

—The company expects an average of 400 on-line transactions per week.

—The expected savings per week should be $20,000.

—The company is open 50 weeks a year.

—The company expects a $1,000,000 savings in year three.

Total three-year savings = 1,750,000

Follow-Up

The company is monitoring the success of the web site and this application. If this is successful, there are other applications they can add to the site. Additionally they are monitoring which customers are accessing the site. Sixty percent of their customers are located in North America, 30% in Europe, 20% in Asia. Depending on demographic use, they will install a mirror web server in their Paris office and in their Singapore office.

Business Case Presentation

Manufacturing Company
On-line Purchasing System

Figure 4-3. Business Case 3

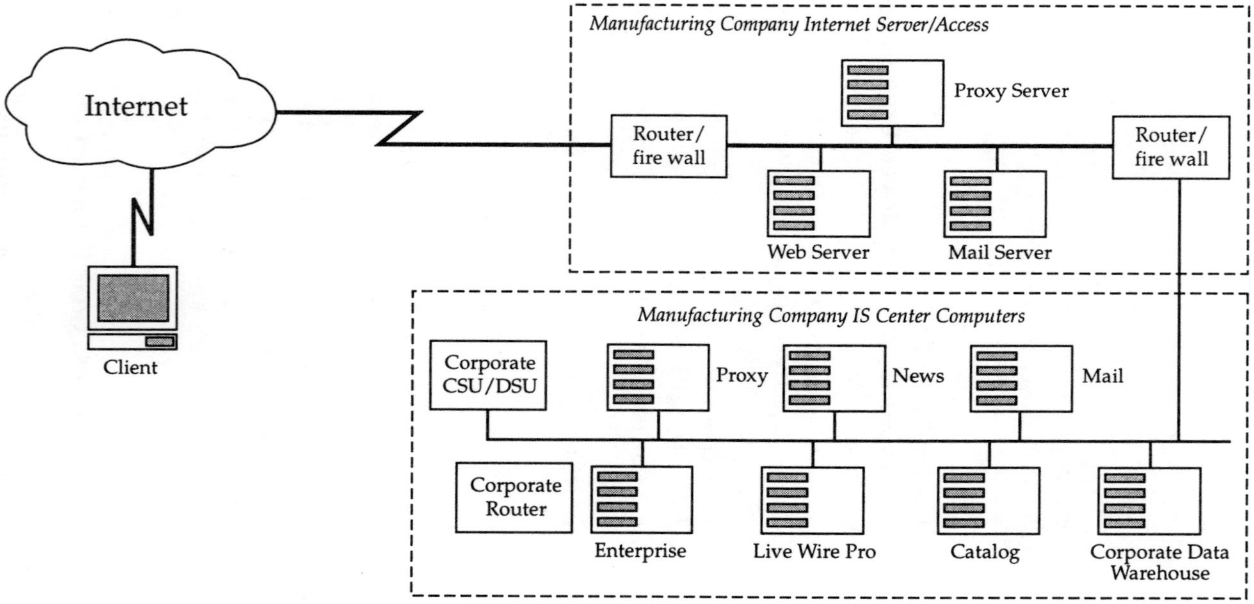

Goal and Benefit

- Create an on-line ordering system for customers.
- Save time and money by automating the ordering process.
- Increase customer satisfaction by increasing communication and providing instant feedback.

Why the Internet

- Easy, low-cost entry
- Worldwide access
- Many tools available for developing application
- Nonintrusive means of providing access to customers
- Application interfaces are straightforward, easy to install, and support customers

Effect on Company

- Internally, little effect on the company.
- Provides sales, manufacturing, and accounting with faster, more accurate information.
- Effectively uses already instituted e-mail.

Cost for Internet Web Access

- $5,000 for fire wall PC
- $35,000 for UNIX web server
- $4,000 for Netscape SuiteSpot
- $25,000 for to write the CGI program
- $5,000 for CSU/DSU
- $1,000 a month, $12,000 a year for communications lines
- $10,000 a year for art and content for the server home page
- $60,000 to train salespeople and customers about the new program
- Year one cost = $156,000
- Three-year cost = $200,000, average cost per year = $66,666

Savings

- Year one savings:
  - —It takes an hour of employee time to process one order.
  - —The average cost per employee is $50.
  - —The company expects an average of 100 on-line transactions per week.
  - —The expected savings per week should be $5,000.
  - —The company is open 50 weeks a year.
  - —The company expects a $250,000 savings in year one.
- Year two savings:
  - —It takes an hour of employee time to process one order.
  - —The average cost per employee is $50.
  - —The company expects an average of 200 on-line transactions per week.
  - —The expected savings per week should be $10,000.
  - —The company is open 50 weeks a year.
  - —The company expects a $500,000 savings in year two.
- Year three savings:
  - —It takes an hour of employee time to process one order.
  - —The average cost per employee is $50.
  - —The company expects an average of 400 on-line transactions per week.
  - —The expected savings per week should be $20,000.
  - —The company is open 50 weeks a year.
  - —The company expects a $1,000,000 savings in year three.
- Total three-year savings = $1,750,000

Time Line

- One month to train internal employees.
- Six months to design, write, and test application.
- Simultaneously six months to create/test technology infrastructure.
- Begin selling application to customers two months before application goes live.
- From approval to live, estimate eight months.

ROI

- Three-year return on this project is 10.86%.
- ROI = cost/profit.
- $190,000/$1,750,000.

Recommendation

- Approve application.
- Approve budget.
- Approve solution.

Scenario 4—Intranet

Developing the Business Case

- *Background.* A regional utility company, employing 10,000 people, is looking at automating and updating some of its internal applications.
- *Customer demographics.* Employees throughout the company have PCs, Macs, or UNIX workstations on their desk. Employees are used to using the computer to access corporate data.
- *Goal.* The company is looking at updating its internal employee application network. Ten years ago the company designed an application that would provide employees with all their office automation needs, including company e-mail, product information, HR information, IS help desk, and room and meeting scheduling. The system was called the Business Automation Software System (BASS).
- *Action.* The company needs to update the BASS application, using infrastructure technology that will be hardware-independent, support future technology, provide easy modular growth, and work with the existing infrastructure. The company is looking at solutions where there is an accessible pool of IS talent and that use modern object-oriented programming technologies.
- *IS infrastructure.* The company has at least one of every kind of computer on the market. The core financial applica-

tions are run on IBM MVS mainframes running CICS and DB2. Around 80% of the company is networked using Ethernet, while the remaining 20% uses token ring or ATM. Satellite offices throughout the main metropolitan area are connected using frame relay. The company has two T3 lines into the main data center. A typical employee is outfitted with a Pentium PC, a color monitor, Microsoft Office, and access to the local file server.

▪ *Solution.* The current infrastructure will be reused. BASS currently runs on UNIX servers. The intent is not to re-create infrastructure but to run the new applications on the current servers. The company wants to phase in the new applications. The company will provide each employee with a web browser. The first phase will be to create an internal home site that departments can use to post pertinent information. The main page of the home site will be for corporate news. There will be a strip at the bottom of the home page listing the other intranet sites employees can visit. Divisions and departments can create their own home page, which employees can access. On the home page there will be an icon that will take employees to the BASS application. When a BASS application is phased out, employees accessing the base site will automatically get taken to the new site that uses intranet technology.

▪ *Architecture/new servers.* The company will maintain the current client-server architecture. The central IS department will maintain the centralized web site. The company will use Netscape server technology. There will be a server dedicated to managing the intranet (Enterprise), Proxy, Mail, News, Catalog, and Live Wire Pro. Each building on the corporate campus will have a mail server and a proxy server. This was decided to keep response times fast. IS will add two PCs to each remote office: one PC will have a local copy of Mail; the other PC will have a local copy of Proxy. All Internet connections will go centrally through IS.

▪ *Security.* This application will work within the company's fire wall and will be independent of any Internet applications.

Cost for Solution

- $340,000 for SuiteSpot per user site licensing price to turn current office automation servers into intranet servers and to put a copy of Netscape Navigator on everyone's desk
- $500,000 to write the first tier of CGI applications
- $20,000 to create an attractive home page template, icons, and departmental templates
- $60,000 for employee training
- Year one cost = $920,000
- Three-year cost = $1,860,000, average cost per year = $620,000

Business Case Presentation

Utility Company
Update Company IS Infrastructure (Intranet)

Goal and Benefit

- Update internal infrastructure.
- Create additional tools for employees to do their job effectively.
- Update current antiquated applications using new, more productive techniques.
- Increase employee productivity by providing timely, easy-to-find information.

Why Use Internet Technology

- Easy, low-cost entry.
- Reuses existing infrastructure.
- Many tools available for developing application.
- Nonintrusive means of providing new application.
- Application interfaces are straightforward, easy to install, and support customers.

Effect on Company

- Logical progression of technology.
- Employees used to accessing information by computer.

Figure 4-4. Business Case 4

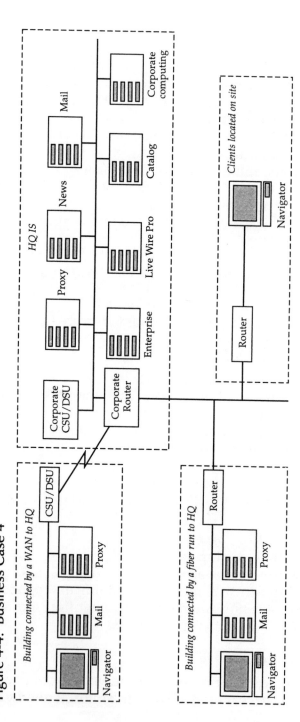

- New applicants will be easier, more intuitive.
- Will need to perform departmental training sessions to increase acceptance.
- Should not increase risk of unwanted intruders accessing corporate records.

Cost for Intranet

- $340,000 for SuiteSpot per user site licensing price to turn current office automation servers into intranet servers and to put a copy of Netscape Navigator on everyone's desk
- $500,000 to write the first tier of CGI applications
- $20,000 to create an attractive home page template, icons, and departmental templates
- $60,000 for employee training
- Year one cost = $920,000
- Three-year cost = $1,860,000, average cost per year = $620,000

Time Line

- One month to train IS employees.
- Six months to design, write, and test first round of applications.
- Simultaneously six months to create/test technology infrastructure.
- One month to train employees.
- Employees can begin accessing the intranet within eight months of executive approval.

Recommendation

- Approve budget.
- Approve solution.

Scenario 5—Small Internet Store

Developing the Business Case

- *Background.* A small local specialty food company, located in a resort town, that packages its own line of specialty condiments and sells products from small local producers. The company is known for its creative gift baskets and interesting assortment of products.

- *Customer demographics.* Urban professionals on vacation looking for picnic supplies or gifts to bring home.

- *Goal.* Owners want to continue living in a resort, but want to expand their selling season beyond the summer months. They have looked into catalog sales and found the cost of entry too high.

- *Action.* The owners have spoken to a local ISP that can support them with web creation, management, and transaction processing. The ISP will charge a flat fee for web site creation and a small fee per transaction. The store already has infrastructure (space and personnel) for storing supplies, creating gift boxes, and shipping gift boxes.

- *IS infrastructure.* The store has a PC and will get a 28.8 modem and a copy of Netscape Navigator Gold. They will receive transaction records with invoice detail from the ISP. They will call the ISP a few times a day and download any transaction information. They will take responsibility for updating web content on a few of the key pages. The key pages will be a section they created called "news from the town," and a "what's new section" details product availability and product description. They have provided the ISP with pictures of the store and products, along with interesting copy. They worked with the ISP web editor to design an interesting and fun flow for people entering the store.

- *Solution.* The site is modeled after the store. The home page is a picture of the front of the store. Clients click on the store, and a picture of the inside of the store appears. A cartoon sales character gives clients a menu of available options. As in the store, customers can decide if they want to have an existing basket or have a custom basket made up for them. Also as in the store, items are grouped in the site under the following categories: deli, condiments, preserves, desserts. Visitors can click on a counter (condiments) and view a row of products, then click on a product and find out all about the product (what it is, how it is used, ingredients, recipes, complementary products). Products can be chosen and placed in a shopping cart or deleted from the cart at any time. On a side column there is a running total that includes item and price. When the customer completes his shopping, he can choose from a variety of gift boxes; he will then be prompted to enter his credit card number, card holder information, and ship-to address. A complete invoice including shipping costs and delivery date is displayed. The customer can approve the order or make changes. For approved orders a copy of the transaction is automatically e-mailed to the customer.

Cost for Solution

- $150 for the Modem
- $79 for Navigator Gold
- $5,000 for ISP to create web site
- $500 setup, $250 per month to maintain the site

Business Case Presentation

Specialty Store
Selling Specialty Products Over the Internet

Goal and Benefit

- Virtual store will provide customers with year-round access.
- Increased market should increase revenues.

Why the Internet

- Easy, low-cost entry.
- Access to larger market.
- Can manage site from current location.
- No big up-front expenditure.

Effect on Company

- Use existing store infrastructure (shipping/receiving/ products).

Figure 4-5. Business Case 5

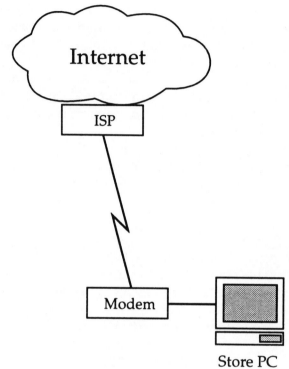

Store PC

- Ability to grow without having to open new stores.
- Access to local residents/future employees if web site takes off.

Cost for Internet

- $150 for the Modem
- $79 for Navigator Gold
- $5,000 for ISP to create web site
- $500 to set up Internet site
- $250 per month, $3,000 a year to maintain Internet site
- Total for first year = $8,729

Time Line

- Three months to design/create site

When the site is producing in the black, the store is looking at increasing staff.

Follow Up

The company is planning on adding a picnic chat line and a recipe chat line. They have begun to add pointers to other products, like wine stores and locations for great picnics. They would like to hire a part-time writer to keep the site looking fresh by adding new, interesting stories. They also would like to hire someone who can answer customer questions.

Technology

In the future they are planning on increasing the network service to their site to include switch 56 (communication line) and add a Proxy NT server. This should increase response times and allow them to add a few more PCs to support the increase in traffic.

Scenario 6—Large Internet Store

Developing the Business Case

- *Background.* Large national store with a large national mail order division.
- *Customer demographics.* Company claims that 95% of the people in the country have been in one of their stores at least once.
- *Goal.* Company wants to maintain market share and market presence. Management feels it is necessary for them to stay in the forefront of merchandising technology.
- *Action.* The company's mail order division will also be responsible for Internet sales.

- *IS infrastructure.* The company currently runs its mail order business on a series of Tandem computers with departmental UNIX file servers and PCs on employees' desks. The company has a T1 to its site and uses TCP/IP to connect all the computers. Phone orders are automatically transmitted to the fulfillment warehouse for shipment.

- *Solution.* The company looks at the Internet as an extension of its current business. Order fulfillment verification and credit card verification will take place on-line while customers are at the site. Processed orders will be sent directly to the warehouse for shipment.

- *Personnel.* The division was planning on upgrading its e-mail system and will accomplish this at the same time the division heads create the web site. They have identified one of their senior UNIX system administrators to become the web master, and have already scheduled people to attend Java, html, and CGI classes. They have also identified a web editor, who is creating a full web content team. The web site will use the already existing product pictures from the mail order catalog. The company plans on taking full advantage of the web's multimedia capabilities, and has begun producing mini-fashion shows for its variety of product lines. The fashion shows will run as movie applets. Clients can click on the fashion icon and a fashion show will play.

Cost for Solution

- $3995 for SuiteSpot
- $950 for merchant systems
- $50,000 for file servers, added T1 lines

Business Case Presentation

Large National Store
Selling Products Over the Internet

Goal and Benefit

- Virtual store will maintain market share, maintain presence.

Figure 4-6. Business Case 6

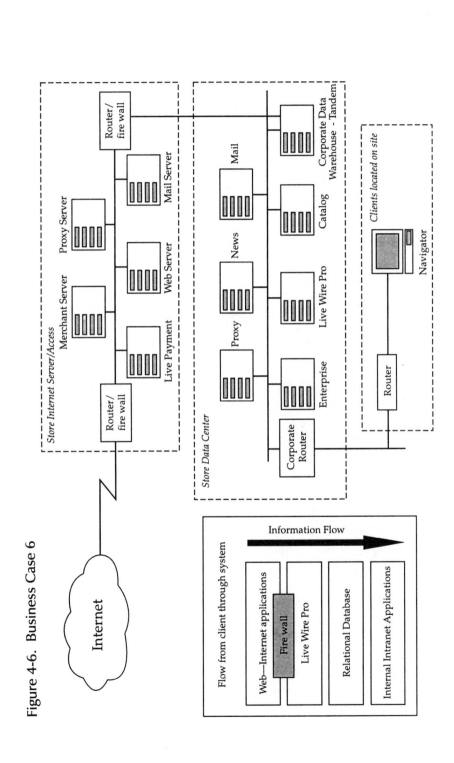

- Will keep company in the forefront of merchandising technology.
- Fits in with CEO's motto: "We go where our customers are."

Why the Internet

- New potential market.
- Access to customers.
- Avoids losing customers to companies that can use Internet's easy access.

Effect on Company

- Uses existing resources.
- Mail order and web order use similar infrastructure.
- Natural progression for business.

Cost for Internet

- $50,000 (budgeted) for new computers
- $10,000 (budgeted) for new software
- $250,000 (budgeted) for new employees
  —Web editor
  —Writer(s)
  —Artist (s)
  —Web traffic manager

Time Line

- Six months to design/create site

Follow-Up

The goal is to make the site a destination location for the buying population. This will be done by creating chat lines to help keep a pulse on the company's audience and to provide a forum to discuss home and personal fashion and by creating a series of on-line fashion and home magazines targeted at the company's Internet audiences. Magazine, feature articles will include live interviews and movie plug-ins.

You should now create a case study, site diagram, and presentation for your concept. Once you have created this presentation you are ready to pitch your idea to the executive staff. Good luck! When they approve your concept, you will be ready to recruit a design team and begin actualizing your web site.

5

Designing Your Internet/Intranet

Depending on the extent of the Internet/intranet you are building, there may be up to four different design processes that you will need to start working on now. Each of the design processes has its own design cycle. Design and development cycles vary in length. All aspects of the design and development will not be simultaneously tracking each other. Designing is similar to cooking dinner on the grill. If you want the grilled vegetables and the chicken to appear on the table at the same time and hot, you need to plan out your dinner. The time it takes and the ingredients it takes to prepare (design) a vegetable dish will be different from the time it takes and the ingredients you will need to prepare chicken. When grilling (development), you don't put tomatoes on the grill at the same time you put chicken on the grill. You need to decide on the intended outcome and plan accordingly. To have everything show up at the right time with the highest quality, you need to plan out when each item will be completed so you can coordinate times.

Identifying the Four Design Processes

1. *Application development* (interactive programs, movies, diagrams). Previously clients were interviewed and an application requirements plan was created. Now a detailed plan of the content requirements is created and reviewed with the client organi-

zation; program flow and access are outlined, the program design is laid out, access to databases is identified and approved; and technology needed for development is identified and purchased.

2. *Web site design* (how people move around the web site). Now the web site flow is flowcharted, content for different client destinations is identified, types of applications are discussed, and an application development cycle begins.

3. *Look and feel* (screen art, icons, fonts, layout). Now the type, size, and nature of borders, banners, page layouts, mascots, pictures, and illustrations are identified.

4. *Designing the Internet/intranet hardware infrastructure* (laying out client server architecture, including LAN, WAN, and Internet access). Now the IS organization reviews its current client-server architecture. The IS organization identifies the company's hardware and network infrastructure currently in place that can be reused for the Internet/intranet applications. Internet/intranet client and server software, new servers, systems that need to be expanded, and sizing for communications lines are identified and ordered.

Overview of the Design Process

During design, IS reviews the estimates they created when the feature list was put together during concept (Chapter 3) and performs an in-depth review and design of each of the features and functionality for the project. The design document that was begun during concept becomes the central IS deliverable. IS management needs to decide what the minimal requirements are for an appropriate design document and what issues are crucial to a project's design. All four of the areas outlined above need to be thought through and designed, and a person needs to be given the responsibility of project managing (project manager) the deliverables through release to clients.

Creating a Good Design

Every project has different needs. There are six standard principles that, if followed, should lead to a good design.

1. *Identify the architect.* Computer legend Fred Brooks says, "Great designs don't come from committees; they come from great designers." It is impossible for multiple people to create a good design. Designate one senior person to be responsible for each area of your Internet/intranet. For large projects the design team may consist of a manager who will go to meetings, a "designer in training" to assist the designer, a person responsible for documenting the design, and a person responsible for developing design tests. Even if the company is designing an item as simple as a home page for the Internet, choose one person to spearhead the design layout, look and feel, and flow from one web page to the next.

2. *Set goals.* Clearly understand what the short- and long-term goals are for the project. A good design allows for future growth. If Microsoft had viewed DOS as a strategic long-term operating system, would they have designed it differently? They did view NT as a long-term strategic operating system and went about designing it very differently from DOS. The same viewpoint should be made with a web design. Understand that departments, divisions, and groups within your organization might want to have their own home page. It looks very unorganized for a large company to have different home pages that are not connected physically or visually. Design your web pages with the understanding that other departments might want to add content or that additional applications might be put up on your web site.

3. *Get perspective on the design.* View the design from many angles. If all the constraints were removed, would the design be different? If so, it is beneficial to reevaluate the design. For example, during the heat of the space race in the 1960s, the U.S. National Aeronautics and Space Administration decided it needed a ball-point pen to write in the zero-gravity confines of its space capsules. After considerable research and development, the astronaut pen was developed at a cost of $1 million. The pen worked and also enjoyed some modest success as a novelty item back here on Earth. The Soviet Union, faced with the same problem, used a pencil.

4. *Don't design in a vacuum.* Designing should be an interactive process. Designers should continually test their design the-

ory. Remember the adage, "How do you eat an elephant? One bite at a time." A practice that will lead to a good design is, Design then test, design then test.

5. *Keep it simple.* Aim for a clean, simple design. If the design is too difficult or too "brilliant," programmers will have a difficult time developing and debugging the application, the IS organization will have a difficult time identifying the cause of problems, and clients will have a hard time navigating through your site.

6. *Don't be "penny-wise and dollar-foolish."* Beware of shortcuts; they rarely save time. Many companies use "freeware" to save time. Since the code was not designed or developed by the company's programmers or by a company that supports their code, the code may be difficult to debug and may not have the necessary features for growth. It is tempting to get free code off of the Internet. Understand that a great benefit of developing or buying code is that you get accountability, reliability, and someone to answer the phone when you get stuck. You have no idea if there was a designer for the free code. Companies that sell products know they need to be competitive and usually can't get funding unless they can prove they have professionals designing, managing, and supporting the technology.

Applications Design

There are many good books on the market that are dedicated to application design. The most important aspects of creating good design are having a clear understanding of what the goal of the application is and understanding the client's needs. This information should have been gathered earlier in the process. Keep in close touch with your client; needs change. Clients can approve a document but find out later they need more functionality. Changes to the design document might not be realistic. It is still good to keep a pulse on these needs. The changes might be minor (e.g., changing a sort field from name to zip code) to major (e.g., needing to connect an Internet application to a database behind a fire wall). It is important to understand where data reside as well as the protections companies place on data.

Larger companies will have documents outlining data flow and requirements to access data. There are many new programs on the market that can be used to create and debug good applications. During design the person(s) responsible for the application should review new development tools and standardize the tools that will be used for this application. Don't get caught in the craze for the latest tool. The tool might not be stable or available in time for your application to go live.

Web Site Design

Web flow is a very important step in creating a successful web site. Web flow combines the talent of laying out a newspaper (content order) with the talent of laying out a town (ease of navigation without getting lost). People like their daily paper because they know exactly what section to go to in order to find the information they want. Sports fans don't need to read the entire paper to get scores for their favorite teams. A good example of easy navigation is Manhattan. Manhattan is set up on a grid system with easily identified streets and avenues. Someone new to New York City should not have a problem figuring out how to get from 73rd to 50th.

You don't want people entering your web site and getting lost in a maze of pages. Use the lead of a newspaper: Organize similar content together under a clearly identifiable heading. Frequent visitors tend to bookmark sites. Keep URLs consistent; don't change the location of a site. Use the lead of a good city planner: Create an easy-to-follow flow, and provide maps that show clients where they are and how to get to where they might want to go.

If clients enter your web site and can't find what they are looking for within the first few pages, they will leave. It is important that you lay out a clear web site that people can easily navigate through and find what they want quickly. If your site is more than ten pages, you will need to create some kind of system to show clients how to navigate through your system. This is similar to maps found at large shopping malls. Some companies who have created nice solutions for ease of navigation are Netscape and Land's End. Netscape incorporates in their web border a locator bar showing how the site is organized, where you are, and allowing you to click on where you want to go. Another solution is Land's End menu-driven access. Land's End provides simple screens, little verbiage, and easy-to-identify banner headlines that take clients directly to a destination. Surf the net to find the sites that have developed a successful way to manage navigating through the web. Show the solutions you like to your web programmer or outside design firm. They can help you create an application that provides simple navigation for your clients.

Look-and-Feel Design

There are also some basic thoughts for designing the look and feel of a web site.

▪ An intranet site does not have to be as pretty or flashy as an Internet site. Decide who the target audience is and design accordingly. For external sites, hire a professional artist; it will make a difference. For your web site design, surf the net, and find a few sites that you like. Either print out the site or bookmark the site. If applicable, show your recommendations to the decision makers or influencers at your company, and get their feedback. When you meet with the designer you can show him the sites you liked and discuss the feedback you received. This will save time and money with your design.

▪ This is a good time to make a policy decision for the company's Internet design. Decide if you want to use one design for the corporate home page, a different design for departmental home pages, and a third design for content pages. Set standards for banners, icons, and font sizes. By setting standards and guidelines up front, you can make the visuals easier for a reader to follow. You may also save time and money in the long run by avoiding having each group design their own web page. If your marketing department has a style guide for your company logo, colors, and fonts, you can have the same style guide created for your web look and feel. The web style guide can reside on-line. The on-line style guide can include sample borders or the mascot in a variety of poses. Decide what kinds of graphics you will

(Text continues on page 118.)

Figure 5-1. Netscape One and Land's End Locators

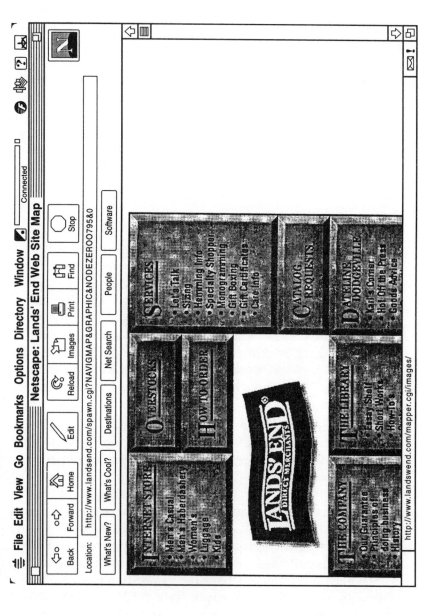

Figure 5-1. (continued)

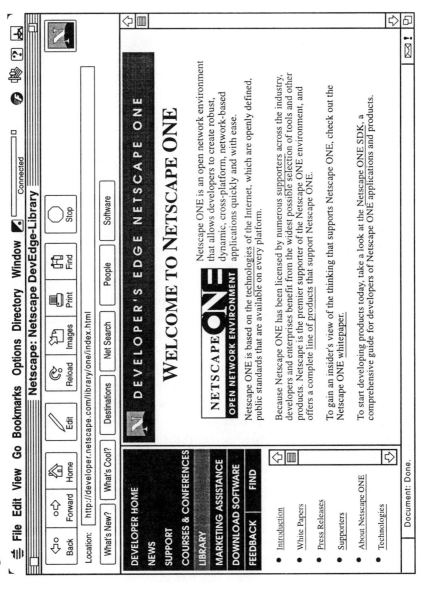

want. Do you want pictures, drawings, or cartoons? You can have a mixture of all these elements, but understand up front what image you want to project. Your company might already have a cartoon mascot. The mascot can be used within your site to illustrate mood, direct clients through the site, or for editorial relief. For instance, if you have integrated a registration screen in your site, you might have your mascot clapping or cheering when a customer completes registration. You can have the mascot pointing the way to interesting destinations. In the example on the next page, Owens-Corning used its pink panther mascot to help clients navigate through its site.

Certain guidelines and standards also apply.

▪ *Set standards for publishing information.* The same way you may have a policy regarding what employees can say to the press or what documents they can give to people outside of the company, you should have a policy on what can be published on a web site. For an Internet an example of web content approval flow may be having a designated person(s) in your marketing organization responsible for publishing web site information. If you have a large site and have hired a web editor, you can set a policy that the editor makes all final decisions on what information is published on your site. You can set a policy that requires any department that wants to publish information on the corporate web site to get approval from a designated person in the organization. The information will then be run past a professional writer. After approval and cleanup the designated web publisher will publish the information. If your company has a large, active site with lots of changing information, you probably will need to hire a team responsible for web publishing. Someone who previously was a magazine editor would be ideal to lead the web content team. Find an editor from a trade publication you like within your industry. It is more important that the editor understand how to write and present to your target market than that he understand the Internet. Your IS team can support the web editor in his effort to manage the technology.

You should also set guidelines for intranet publishing. If

Figure 5-2. Owens-Corning Mascot

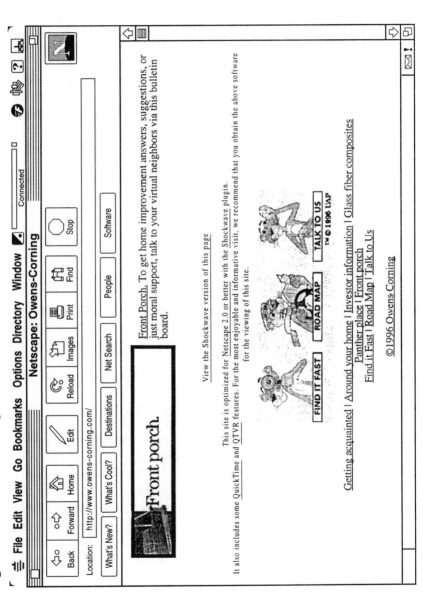

File Edit View Go Bookmarks Options Directory Window

Netscape: Owens-Corning

Back | Forward | Home | Edit | Reload | Images | Print | Find | Stop

Location: http://www.owens-corning.com/

What's New? | What's Cool? | Destinations | Net Search | People | Software

Front porch.

Front Porch. To get home improvement answers, suggestions, or just moral support, talk to your virtual neighbors via this bulletin board.

View the Shockwave version of this page

This site is optimized for Netscape 2.0 or better with the Shockwave plugin. It also includes some QuickTime and QTVR features. For the most enjoyable and informative visit, we recommend that you obtain the above software for the viewing of this site.

FIND IT FAST | ROAD MAP | TALK TO US
™ © 1996 TAP

Getting acquainted l Around your home l Investor information l Glass fiber composites
Panther place l Front porch
Find it Fast l Road Map l Talk to Us

© 1996 Owens-Corning

employees are publishing confidential documents, you may want to design a screen format that has the word *confidential* embedded in the background. Department heads should set policy on what can be published, as well as quality standards for publishing internal documents. You might want to place confidential corporate documents behind a password protection. That way you can provide easy access to documents for a controlled group of people. An intranet is available to everyone in your company. When publishing information on an internal web page, ask the question, "If the CEO stumbles onto this page, will heads roll?" A question like this should provide most people with a benchmark for appropriate behavior.

▪ Set guidelines for e-mail. Understand that e-mail messages are written documents that can be easily forwarded to unknown parties. If you have salespeople communicating with customers, make sure they don't e-mail information they wouldn't put in a letter. There have been instances of employees sending "flame e-mail" to a writer of an article they didn't like. Since the e-mail was sent using the company's e-mail address, the reporter can consider this flame mail an official company document. Setting clear policy on what type of information can be sent outside the company will hopefully save the company an embarrassing situation.

Site Design

For all but the smallest companies a comprehensive site plan should exist. Site plans typically come in two formats: physical and logical. The physical plan displays the building layout, wiring plan, types of connections from desktop to the wiring closet, types of connections within a wiring closet, location of file servers, connections between file servers, and connections between the outside world and the company.

A logical plan shows what work groups are connected to what servers and printers, and how work groups connect to corporate resources. Since Internet/intranet applications work within existing client-server environments, the physical plan does not need to be modified. The logical plan will need to be

Figure 5-3. Physical Design

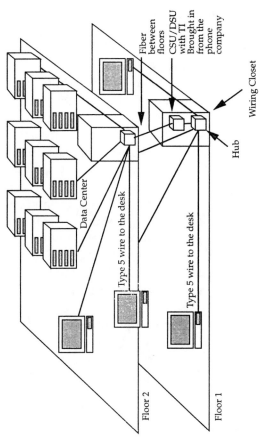

Fiber between floors

CSU/DSU with T1 Brought in from the phone company

Wiring Closet

Hub

Data Center

Type 5 wire to the desk

Type 5 wire to the desk

Floor 2

Floor 1

modified, since a group of new servers will be added and clients will need access to these servers.

The member of your IS team who is responsible for the logical layout will need to work with the web master to provide corporate-wide connections to the new intranet servers. For an Internet, you will need to figure out how many hits you think your server will receive so that you can provide adequate hardware and communication lines. For example, a high-end NT PC supporting passive applications can support around 1,000,000 hits a day when connected to a T1 line. If you are planning on hosting a web site, you will need to estimate how active you think your web site will be and decide how database-intensive your applications will be. A system that can easily support 1,000,000 passive hits will not be able to support very many hits if the application is a movie. When you buy a server to support a specific application (passive site, transaction site, movie site), the vendor should be able to provide you with performance data. Another good source for performance data is computer magazines. Editors are continually running special benchmark sections using the latest software. Surf the Internet. If you find a web site that has a similar application to what you are planning on running, e-mail the web master. After telling him how much you like his site, ask how many hits a day the site is supporting and what hardware and software it is running.

Security decisions need to be decided and laid out at this time. For intranets the company should already have a comprehensive security plan. For new Internets additional security will need to be created. There are a few basic forms of security available. Companies can pick and choose what form of security meets the needs of their site. Security comes in both hardware and software. Hardware solutions include fire walls, while software solutions include authentication and encryption.

The most basic form of security is a fire wall. Fire walls are a combination of computers and routers placed between the outside world (telecommunications line) and the company's computers. A fire wall filters all data, checking to make sure the information transmitted does not include viruses, illegal cookies, or other unwanted transmissions. Companies can design their fire wall in a number of configurations. If a company has

Figure 5-4. Logical Design

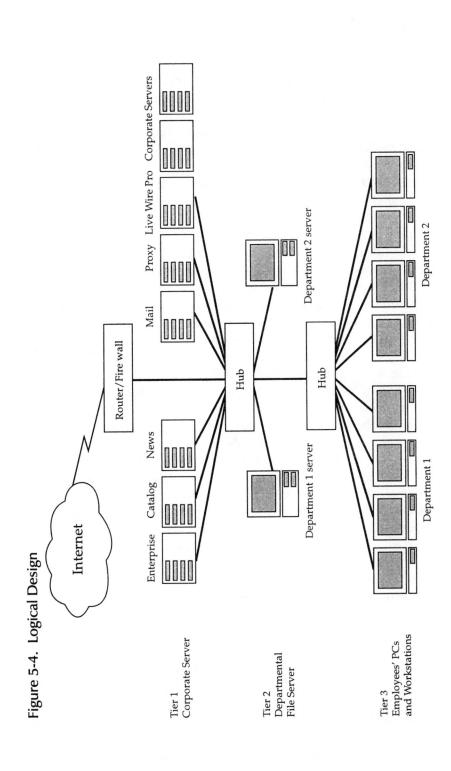

data it wants to keep secure from any intruders, it can create a fire wall that completely blocks access. Or a company can "punch holes" in a fire wall, allowing special applications to break through to access data. If you are using your site to support a customer application, you might want to punch a hole in your fire wall. That way a customer can provide you with his customer number and you can display the customer's information. The Internet application goes through the fire wall hole to get the customer information from a secure server. Companies that are running applications that do a lot of transactions may want to put a machine outside the fire wall that has limited customer information. That way clients don't need to continually break through the fire wall. Some companies employ dual fire wall systems. The first fire wall checks to make sure the transmission is legal. A series of computers that support the web site are placed inside this fire wall; then a second fire wall is placed between the web site and the company. It is virtually impossible for an illegal intruder to navigate through two fire walls.

In a two-fire-wall configuration a company will place one mail server between the fire walls and another inside the site. All mail from the outside world will be stored on the mail server between the fire walls. All mail going to the outside world will be stored on the fire wall inside the company. Periodically the mail server inside will check the mail for viruses and then send the mail to the mail server between the fire walls. Periodically the mail server between the fire walls will check the Internet for its company's mail and transmit it to the outside. The mail received from the outside world will be checked for viruses. If the mail is clean, the mail server between the fire walls will transmit the mail to the mail server inside the company. Because the information transmission is staged and all transfers are checked, it is virtually impossible for an intruder to break through or corrupt data.

Authentication and encryption are two of many means available to support secure software environments. Authentication is a process where a client signs on to a system and is given a token that identifies what he has access to. Each application or computer checks to make sure the client has a valid token before allowing him to pass. Encryption takes the information being

Figure 5-5. Secure Mail Transfer

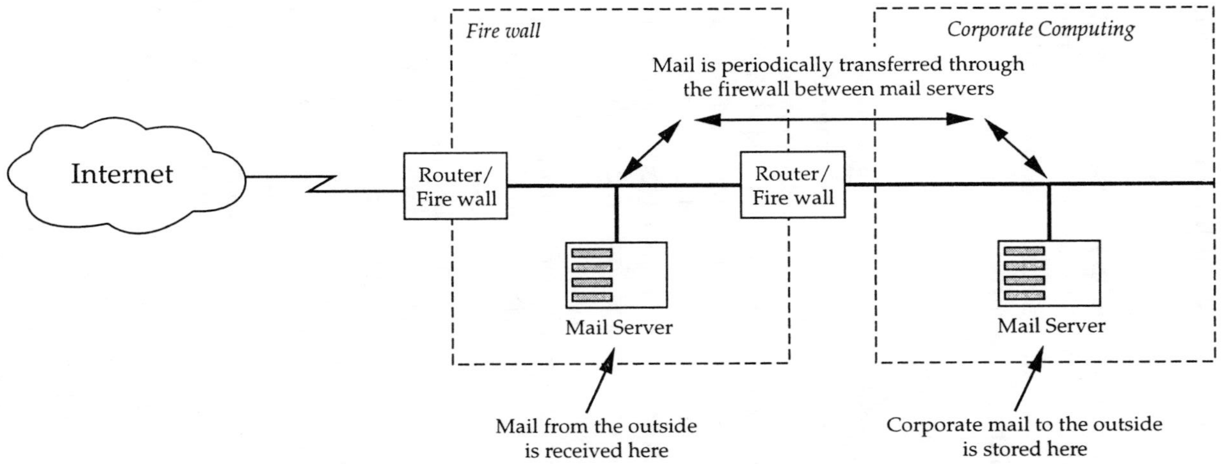

Corporate Computing

Mail is periodically transferred through
the firewall between mail servers

Fire wall

Router/
Fire wall

Router/
Fire wall

Mail Server

Mail Server

Internet

Corporate mail to the outside
is stored here

Mail from the outside
is received here

transmitted (e.g., credit card number) and changes it to a string of incomprehensible characters. The only way the string can be turned back into its original form is if it is received by a computer that has the encryption key for that particular transmission.

The web master and IS representative responsible for managing the site will need to design an infrastructure including a security system that will provide the company with the maximum flexibility and security.

Reviewing the Design

As each design element is completed, it is important to hold a design review. A design review is a meeting where people who are experienced in the element created review the design (an element may be a program, layout, site design, or security design). Design reviews confirm that the design is reasonable, obtainable, efficient, and realistic. If the company is small or all the experts in that particular area were used to design the document, it is recommended that an outside expert(s) who has yet to see the design be brought in to review the design. Take the time to bring in a fresh person to review the design. Changes now may save lots of grief and money in the future.

Many projects hit snags in development, quality assurance, and beta testing (a prereleased system is given to a group of clients to confirm it works properly) after they are released because the people designing the project did not have the opportunity to have an objective professional review the design document and confirm that the design was appropriate before development began. No matter what the size of the project, a design flaw found up front saves money down the line. Guidelines need to be developed in order to have successful design reviews.

Most people are threatened by design reviews. People may have spent months designing a project. They resent an outsider reviewing what they have done. Don't let this resistance stop your company from reviewing the design. Don't let an employee's status cause you to waive this requirement. Senior people can also overlook things. An experienced designer may be used as an example of how to create a good design for junior employ-ees. To make design reviews a positive experience, the following steps are recommended:

- Apply design reviews to everyone. Singling out a person or a group creates bad feelings.
- Provide the person with a list of what will be looked for in advance. This helps the people on the review panel and the people being reviewed.
- Establish with the designer and the review panel the pur-pose of this review.
- Provide a neutral facilitator.
- Make this an enjoyable process. An employee can show that he is senior by coming in with a well-thought-out complete design.

It is necessary for the IS/marketing organization to identify what the review panel will be looking for. For instance, the com-pany is developing a series of CGI applications to facilitate cus-tomer ordering. The programmers will know they will be asked to show ease of use and screen layout, access to existing data-bases, and where information resides in context to the fire wall. The programmers will know in advance what questions will be asked. Anticipating these questions will assist the person pre-senting the design group to identify how to present the design. If the application includes accessing databases held by different departmental servers, a good idea would be to identify the servers needing to be accessed and identify the person responsi-ble for approving this access.

The same principle applies for reviewing a web site design. It is worth the time to find a web consultant or media publisher to review the flow of information. It's easy to get lost in a web site. A web site design review should focus on confirming that the site flows smoothly, consistently, and correctly. Keep the project goal in mind. You should have a clear idea what message you want your web site to articulate. The same time and energy should be spent reviewing an intranet. You don't want employ-ees lost within your company's web site. Intranets don't need to be as visually stunning or exciting as Internets. Intranets still need to get employees to their destination easily and to have functioning navigation tools. A poorly laid out intranet with no navigation aids is a disaster in the making. Bad Internet layout gets few repeat customers; bad intranet layout results in employees complaining loudly.

QA and Documentation

It is wise to appoint someone up front who will be responsible for making sure the application or Intranet/intranet works as specified in the requirements document. This person is typically referred to as *quality assurance* (QA). Even if the site or application is very small or simple, it is a good idea to have fresh eyes review the site and confirm it does what the requirements document claims. Make sure this person understands his responsibility to quality-assure a product and takes this responsibility seriously. A QA person should be responsible for making sure a client can easily move through the site, ensuring that instructions are easy to understand and checking that information is accurate, that there are no typos, that pointers go to the correct place, and that icons and pictures are accurate and appropriate. If the company is implementing a full-blown solution using all four elements outlined earlier in this chapter, a small team of QA people can make sure all the elements work together.

Documentation

Some projects will need documentation. Depending on the project, documentation might be simple or complex. Don't leave the documentation to the programmers or web designers. Take the time to hire a professional writer. Documentation might be a booklet given to each employee explaining the Intranet/intranet and highlighting functions and sites that can be visited. Alternatively the documentation might be a series of on-line pull-down help screens to help clients navigate through the web site or work a specific application.

Near the end of the design process the person responsible for QA and the documentation writer are brought in to review the design document and are invited to the design review meeting. QA and the writer are each responsible for developing a document that will outline what their deliverables will look like and to provide their capital, resource, and time needs to the person managing the project. A good rule of thumb is to estimate that QA and the writer will each use twenty-five percent of the time and cost it will take for a programmer to develop the application. For instance, if it will take $100,000 and six months to design an application, budget two months and $25,000 for QA and a writer. The programmer or web designer will need to assist QA and the writer in their efforts to create their plans for the site.

Help Desk Role

In most companies the help desk is responsible for working with employees who have IS questions. Your intranet site should be supported by your company's help desk. The project manager should get a member of the help desk staff appointed to the team of people designing your Internet/intranet. Getting a help desk member on the team will help cut support problems after the applications are released. The help desk representative should be responsible for looking at the product being developed to identify any special needs the client may have. Having a help desk employee on the team helps facilitate information within the IS organization. A help desk representative can give good feedback regarding what the department will need to learn, as well as offer support and identify problems once the project is released. Help desk employees need to review the design document and client documentation to ensure that features to support clients will be tested the way they perceive those features to be used. They will confirm that the documents will provide the level of information necessary so that clients can download, understand, and use the applications with little support. The easier the application is to use, the more independent the client will be. An independent client uses fewer company resources than a dependent client. It is worthwhile to put time and energy in up front in development in order to create a project that will be easily supported once released. Help desk management is aware of the cost advantage of developing a project that allows for client independence; they are responsible for championing easy-to-use features and usable documentation. Help desk needs to review their organization's ability to service the product and identify what changes are needed to make the organization more efficient and effective in supporting clients.

Similarly you should have an organization responsible for supporting Internet clients. The type of web site applications you have will define the type of Internet support organization you will need. If you have a passive web site or you are selling product(s) on your web site, your Internet support organization most likely will be marketing or salespeople responsible for answering customer e-mail inquiries. If you have applications on your web site, you will need to have people who can answer questions on using these applications. The organization responsible for supporting a web site should be aware that they have this responsibility and should be brought in early so they can make sure they understand the requirements this will pose.

After the design review, IS should have a concrete plan of what they will create, when it will be created, and when it will be completed. Once documentation, QA, and help desk have had the opportunity to identify and document their needs and resources, the person responsible for managing the product creates an integrated schedule.

Creating an Integrated Schedule

After designing your Internet/intranet you will need to put together a realistic schedule and clearly define the cost of this project. Hopefully you properly padded your budget, since there are always hidden costs. The first order of business is to create an integrated schedule. If done properly this tool will provide you with an accurate date by which the project will be completed. One commonly used method to create an integrated schedule is to have each of the team members provide the project manager with each member's schedule. If the project manager creates an integrated schedule without an interactive forum, there is no buy-in, opportunity to examine disconnects, or team understanding of handoffs and prerequisites. A better method is for the project manager to facilitate an interactive forum where each member of the product team presents deliverables and prerequisites. An interactive forum usually consists of a half-day session. In an interactive forum it becomes obvious where there are disconnecting schedules.

To run an interactive session the project manager asks a representative from each element, the QA, the writer, and help desk support to break deliverables down by action item. Each deliverable has an end date, begin date, or both. Departmental representatives put all their deliverables up on a board. Have the team members write their information on Post-its; that way they can move their action item around the board to create a PERT chart organized by date. A good exercise is to have each team member fill out a Post-it for each of his activities.

In the center of the Post-it have the team member identify the activity. On the right-hand corner, have the team member write the number of days needed to complete this activity. Give each Post-it a unique number. Place the number in the left-hand corner. Have the team members place their Post-its on a wall in chronological order. After everyone puts their Post-it on the wall, have the team members find any prerequisite Post-it activities. Have them place the prerequisite number in the lower right-hand corner of the Post-it. You have now created a paper-integrated PERT schedule of your project. The project manager can now create a computer version of this PERT chart (there are quite a few good project management software applications that can be used). The integrated schedule is a tool that can be used to correctly gauge the level of expectation of product develop-

Figure 5-6. Post-It

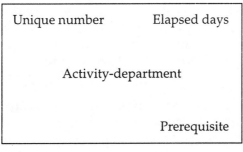

ment, identify an accurate release date, identify critical path deliverables, identify departments' prerequisites, understand where schedule slips might occur, and monitor the progress of the product through its life cycle.

One common mistake in creating an integrated schedule is for the team to be told when deliverables must be completed. Don't succumb to creating a schedule based on a delivery date. Allow the team to build an integrated schedule based on how long they think tasks will take. If the schedule does not meet a prerequisite date, a realistic schedule will be needed so that the team can figure out realistic changes. There are many things a team can do to shorten the development time without misrepresenting the time it takes to accurately complete a task. With a realistic schedule that needs to be shortened, the team can better assess risk. The team can identify what tasks may be performed simultaneously or earlier, where extra resources can be added to minimize time, and what features, if minimized, will decrease development time. For a very tight schedule, projects can be broken apart and released in two phases, allowing a less feature-rich but properly tested application or web site to go live on time. After a realistic integrated schedule is available, the team needs to provide its budget to the project manager so a baseline cost document can be created.

Creating a Baseline Cost Document

It is the responsibility of the project manager to create a baseline cost document. This document is used to itemize all costs attributed to this project. The baseline cost document provides management with an accurate picture of the real cost of the project, along with accurate detail for creating accounting documents such as an ROI analysis. There are four subcategories of costs that people working on the project need to provide to the project manager: staffing, external and internal capital requirements, material requirements, and other direct costs. The project manager needs to work with each of the product team members to get his costs so that the document can be completed.

Staffing requirements. Each person needs to provide the project manager with information on any specific staffing require-

(Text continues on page 139.)

Figure 5-7. Post-It Exercise

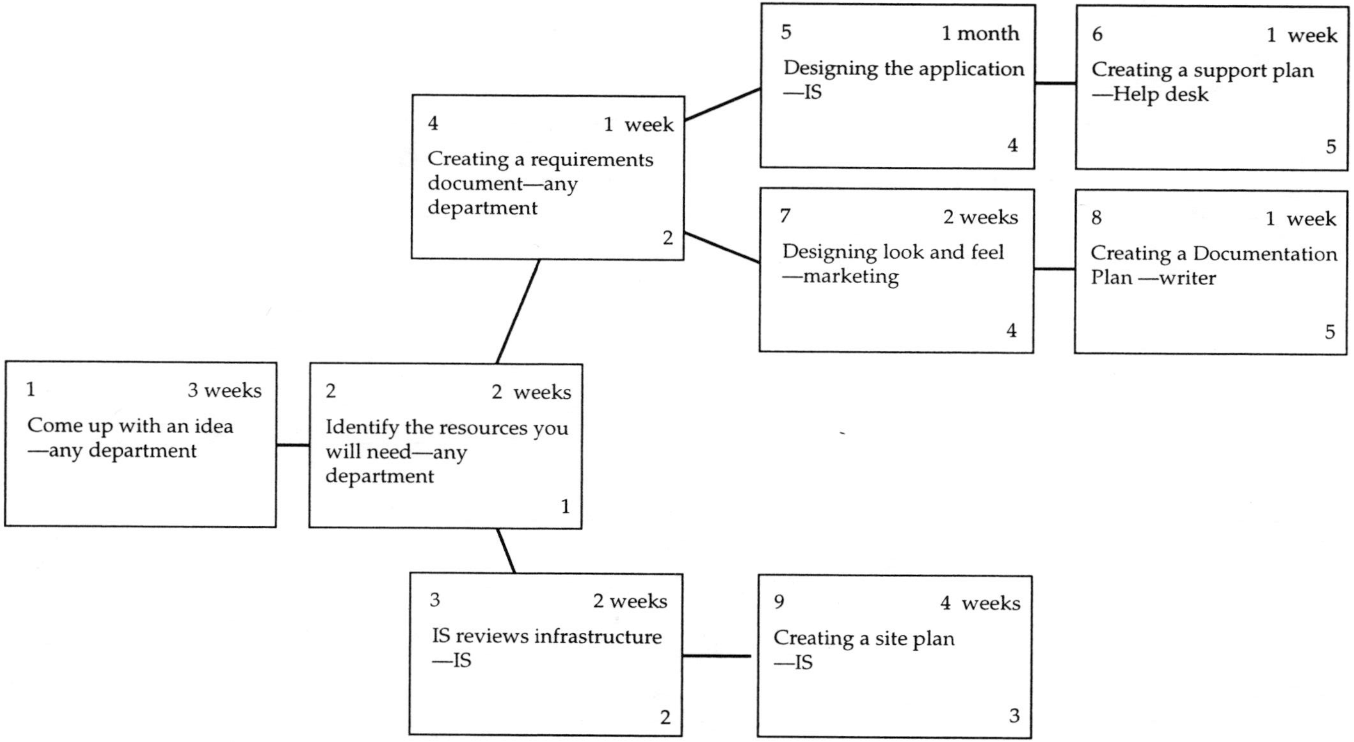

1 | 3 weeks
Come up with an idea
—any department

2 | 2 weeks
Identify the resources you
will need—any department
1

4 | 1 week
Creating a requirements
document—any
department
2

3 | 2 weeks
IS reviews infrastructure
—IS
2

5 | 1 month
Designing the application
—IS
4

6 | 1 week
Creating a support plan
—Help desk
5

7 | 2 weeks
Designing look and feel
—marketing
4

8 | 1 week
Creating a Documentation
Plan —writer
5

9 | 4 weeks
Creating a site plan
—IS
3

Figure 5-8. Baseline Cost

Program: Project LIFE CYCLE

Organization: DEVELOPMENT COST BASELINE STAFFING REQUIREMENTS*

Prepared by: (Man months per Quarter)

Date: 10/9/97

Page:__1__of__5

Item #	Labor Type	Task Description	Name	FY Plant (Yes/No)	F95				F96				F97		
					Q1	Q2	Q3	Q4	Q1	Q2	Q3	Q4	Q1	Q2	Q3

Man hours

Man months

Total man months 0   0 0 0 0 0 0 0 0 0 0 0 0 0 0

*173 hours per man month
(This document provides detailed information on employee costs by project)

Program:
Organization:
Prepared by:

Project LIFE CYCLE
DEVELOPMENT COST BASELINE CAPITAL REQUIREMENTS
(Internal Equipment)

Item #	Description	Qty.	Program Usage (%)	Cap./ Qty.	Usage Start Date (mm/yy)	Asset #	Existing Acq. Date (Qtr/FY)	Standard Cost	New Acq. Date (Qtr/FY)	Unit Cost	Usage End Date†

†Return date, dedicated (DED) or spares (SP)
(This document provides detailed information on cost of internally developed hardware or software to develop this project)

(continues)

Figure 5-8. (continued)

Program:

Prepared by:

Project LIFE CYCLE
DEVELOPMENT COST BASELINE
CAPITAL REQUIREMENTS

Date: 10/9/97
Page:__3__of__5

Item #	Description	Qty.	Program Usage (%)	Usage Start Date	Asset #	Existing	Purchase Price	New		Usage End Date†
				(mm/yy)		Acq. Date (Qtr/FY)		Acq. Date (Qtr/FY)	Unit Cost	

†Return date or dedicated (DED)
(This document provides detailed information on cost of purchasing hardware or software to develop this project)

Program:
Organization:
Prepared by:

Date:

Project LIFE CYCLE
DEVELOPMENT COST BASELINE
MATERIAL REQUIREMENTS*

Item #	Description	Purchase Date (Qtr/FY)	Unit of Measurement	Qty	Unit Price	Total Price

*Material is less than $1,000 and has a useful life of less than two years (usually scrapped at the end of development) (This document provides detailed information on cost of purchasing materials to develop this project)

(continues)

Figure 5-8. (continued)

Program:
Organization:
Prepared by:

Date:
Page:___5__of___5

Project LIFE CYCLE
DEVELOPMENT COST BASELINE
OTHER DIRECT COST REQUIREMENTS*

Item #	Company Name	Task Description	Period of Service†	Estimated Total Price

*Outside laboratories, testing facilities, consulting, licensing fees, leasing company, travel, etc.
†Start date (QTR/FY) and length of service
(This document provides detailed information on cost not already included to develop this project)

ments. Staffing requirements detail information on the number of employee hours it will take to produce this product. The information necessary to identify is the employee's status (consultant, part-time, full-time, or exempt), the employee's department and position (e.g., writer or editor), name of each employee, whether this person is included within the department's existing fiscal plan, and the amount of hours this employee will be working on this project by quarter.

External and internal capital requirements. To develop a product, sometimes additional equipment needs to be purchased or capital needs to be associated with the project. Capital requirements provide detail on capital and equipment either found internally or purchased. It is necessary for each department to identify the capital item, the percentage of this resource the project will use (for a person this would be the percentage of their time; for capital this would be the percentage used up, or the percentage in use), whether the company will capitalize the equipment, the date the company will begin to use the item, the capital-identifying number, the company assigned to this equipment, the date the product was acquired, the cost of purchasing components or internal cost of capital, and the date the project will stop using this equipment.

Material requirements. Material requirements detail information on the cost of purchasing materials that are under $1,000 and have a useful life of less than two years. It is necessary to identify each line item by department, date the company took possession of the materials, standard unit of measurement, quantity purchased, price for each unit, and total price.

Other direct costs. Other direct costs are items not detailed in the previous sections. Items such as hiring a public relations firm, printing cost, and advertising fall under this category. Identify the name of the company, the item or service that is being purchased from this company, how the item or service will be used, the length of time this item or service will be used, and the estimated price of this item or service.

Strategic Agreements

Many products are developed using commercial software technology. Software companies may provide development platforms separately from client licensing agreements. It is the project manager's responsibility to confirm that client license agreements are in place. The project manager brings the details of the contract information to the team so they can confirm that their plans meet with the outside agreements. IS management needs to make sure that the project manager is given access to any contract sessions and put on any contract approval list.

Summary

Now the team has designed the project, decided scope of documentation and quality assurance, and estimated the time to develop the application and the cost of creating the application. The actual information at this stage should be laid out and presented to the executive staff. The presentation should be simple. For example, if scenario four (the utility company) from Chapter 4 is the project and the team finds out that they were on target, it is good to highlight this. If there is a change to the estimated costs or availability date, it is necessary to track the change and highlight the effect of the change.

Presentation to Executive Staff
Utility Company

Update company IS infrastructure (intranet)
Update to presentation given (date)

Goal and Benefit

- Update internal infrastructure
- Create additional tools for employees to do their job effectively
- Update current antiquated applications using new, more productive techniques
- Increase employee productivity by providing timely, easy-to-find information

Internet Solution

- *Purpose:* To provide customers with on-line ordering and tracking
- *Proposal estimates:*
  Estimated three-year cost at proposal time: $190,000
  Estimated three-year savings at proposal time: $1,750,000
  Estimated time for completion: 6 months
- *Design estimates:*
  Current 3-year cost at design time: $195,000
  Estimated 3-year savings at design time: $1,750,000
  Estimated time for application availability: 7 months

Original Cost for Solution

- $5,000 for fire wall PC
- $35,000 for UNIX web server
- $4,000 for Netscape SuiteSpot
- $25,000 to write the CGI program
- $5,000 for CSU/DSU
- $1,000 a month, $12,000 a year for communications lines
- $10,000 a year for art and content for the server home page
- $60,000 to train salespeople and customers about the new program
  Year 1 cost = $145,000
- Three-year cost = $190,000, average cost per year = $63,334

Cost Update at Design

- $5,000 for fire wall PC
- $35,000 for UNIX web server
- $4,000 for Netscape SuiteSpot
- $30,000 to write the CGI program
- $5,000 for CSU/DSU
- $1,000 a month, $12,000 a year for communications lines
- $10,000 a year for art and content for the server home page

- $60,000 to train salespeople and customers about the new program
- Year 1 cost = $145,000
- Three-year cost = $190,000, average cost per year = $63,334

Change Report

- Change from proposal is $5,000 for CGI application.
- There will be a one-month slip in the project.
- Reasons:
    —Additional cost will be incurred, since scripts will need to be written. These scripts will provide fast access to information from existing databases while securing the database behind the company's fire wall.
    —Slip is due to unavailability of hardware, software, and dataphone lines. Slip includes the time it will take to get this infrastructure working properly.

Now that the design has been approved and the changes reviewed, you are ready to develop the web site or intranet.

6

Developing and Testing Your Internet/Intranet Site

After designing your site you will need to implement the design. As discussed in Chapter 5 there are up to four different cycles you might be going through now. The four cycles that were outlined in design and are created in development are: application development, web site design, look and feel, and hardware infrastructure design.

For each of the four areas being developed, the people responsible for developing that area take their respective design document and create the actual solution. For example, programmers will take a design document and write code to the specifications outlined. As hardware and software arrives the people responsible for systems configure the systems and optimize the network. The web master is setting up the web servers and obtaining a unique domain name. The web editor has created an extensive flowchart of the web site. As he receives web content he confirms that the content meets corporate quality standards and begins linking sites based on the flowchart. As banners, icons, and illustrations become available, these elements are added to the web content. As applications become available the web editor confirms that these applications are linked to the appropriate place within the site. Large web sites are very dynamic; design to development may be an ongoing process. The web site design/development/publishing process is similar to magazine or newspaper publishing. Web site publishing differs from standard print media publishing in that the content for web publishing will be electronically "published" (transmitted) to the web server instead of transmitted to paper.

It is wise to stage applications and web sites on different servers. One server can be set aside for development (putting everything together). When the programmer completes the application or the web editor completes the web site, the completed project is electronically moved to a quality assurance/test/beta computer. Once approved and completed the project can then be moved to a "live" computer. Physically separating out the three main phases of development and creating a sign-off procedure before content gets moved to the next system will save confusion in the long run. There are many stories of people getting confused and putting development or beta information on a system that can be accessed by clients. Planning procedures up front saves confusion in the long run. For large sites that will need a three-phase approach, a person should be designated the release engineer. A release engineer is the single point of contact responsible for moving information from one system to the next system. Creating a formal procedure will save confusion and embarrassing problems.

Web Development

During development, artist or design teams are hired to create an appropriate look and feel for the site. The look and feel is developed to match the client with the project. The figure on the next two pages shows two companies that set up their site design similarly. They both have a home site locator set up as a destination. Burton's snowboard site is set up like a ski resort; Lexus's site is set up like a concert hall. The articulation of the sites differs drastically. Burton's copy mirrors the expressions used by their young, "radical" snowboard clientele, whereas the Lexus automobile site exudes an expensive, elegant look and feel that matches the mature, upscale Lexus client.

The look and feel takes into account design, typeface, back-

Figure 6-1. Lexus, Burton Web Site Home Page

(continues)

Figure 6-1. (continued)

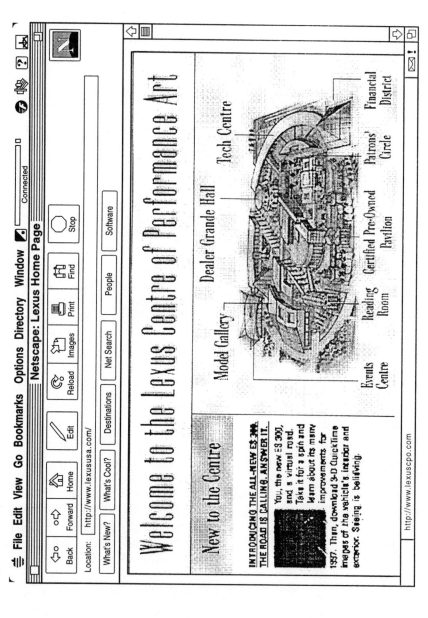

ground, and display format. Your design documents should provide the artist with a good idea of what your target audience is like. You should have decided in design if you want a site mascot, illustrations, or photographs. This way the artist or design team will design web content that will match your image. After the images or templates are approved, they can be integrated into your web pages. For large sites a pasteup board where printed content pages can be laid out in flowchart order can be helpful. It can get confusing to create the web site PERT chart and make sure content moves smoothly from one place to another. Physically printing out pages helps people work the flow visually.

Development Review

Web sites and applications need to go through a review before being handed off to QA. This is another stage that companies frequently overlook. The same people who assisted in the design review should be asked back to the development review. The purpose of the development review is to make sure the project developed meets the design specifications and meets the quality requirements of the company. This includes making sure that code and artwork were not obtained illegally. There are many horror stories of sites developed, tested, and released and then the company being sued because there were questions regarding ownership.

Development reviews are similar to design reviews in that guidelines need to be developed in order to have a successful development review. Most people are as threatened by development reviews as they are by design reviews. Developers may spend a year working on a project. They resent an outsider reviewing what they have done. Don't let this resistance stop the company from reviewing the project. Don't let an employee's status cause you to waive this requirement. Senior people can also overlook things. Keep the reviews informal; the purpose is not to beat people up but to confirm that the application or site works. To make development reviews a positive experience, the following six ideas are recommended:

Figure 6-2. Web Site Layout

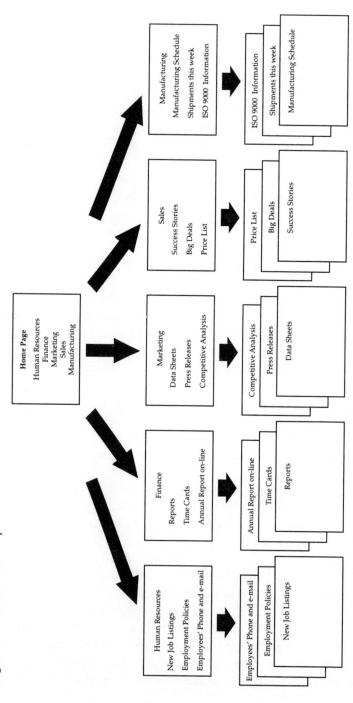

1. Apply design reviews to everyone. Singling out people or groups creates bad feelings.
2. Provide the presenter with a list of what will be looked for in advance. This helps the people on the review panel as well as the people being reviewed.
3. Discuss with the presenter and the review panel the purpose of this review.
4. Give the presenter time to make corrections after the development review.
5. Provide a neutral facilitator.
6. Make this an enjoyable process. An employee can show that he is senior by coming in with a nicely executed project.

Setting Severity Levels

Companies typically have a grading system whereby anyone notifying the help desk of a bug can identify the severity of that bug. For instance, the severity rating can run from 1 to 5, 1 being the worst. A severity-1 bug would notify the company that the bug crashes the system, while a severity-5 bug could mean that punctuation in a message is incorrect. The web editor, QA, help desk, and IS need to review the severity rating system and make sure they agree on what types of errors fall into which categories. Setting severity levels up front will help the creators identify the severity of a problem and prioritize their response. A creator will fix a severity-1 system crash problem before fixing a severity-5 punctuation problem.

Writer

The writer uses the documentation plan developed during design as the basis for writing the documentation. The programmer, the web master, or the web editor provides the writer with the outline document detailing what he has created or needs to have explained. The person developing the application provides the writer with access to early code so that the writer can review the application and write appropriate documentation. The web editor provides the writer with early access of screens so that the writer can document any necessary help information. The writer presents his first draft documentation to the team for review. The team members are responsible for confirming that the first-draft documentation meets the needs of their department and the documentation plan. The first-draft changes should be returned and the documentation updated before QA begins. The web editor will need to coordinate and map out what pull-down menus will be accessible at which screen. An intranet site browser can be customized to include information necessary for employees to work more efficiently.

The team should now have a completed project waiting to be tested and a first-draft document from the writer. QA is now on the critical path. During this phase QA begins testing the project in earnest. QA must test the project in accordance with the description of how the project will be used by the client as defined in the requirements document and the QA test plan presented to the team. One of the tests that QA performs is to access the application or site and run through a simulated use of the project as if QA were an actual client. This test includes using the documentation and using a system that would be configured like that of the average client. Any errors, problems, or recommendations that QA identifies are documented and logged. It is important for QA to run through a simulated client procedure and projected-use scenario, since it is in the best interest of the company to have a site that is not only error-free but easy to use and navigate through. The cost savings to support a site that works makes up for any inconveniences, as well as the time it takes to properly test a site.

A QA person responsible for verifying a web site should look for the following items:

- Imbedded pointers and URLs send people to the correct screen.
- Clients are not dropped off into error code screens.
- Site navigation is easy and straightforward; clients don't get lost in a site maze.
- Screen content matches screen banners.

- It doesn't take more than two screens for a client to get where he wants to go.
- Site looks professional—no misspellings, typos, or punctuation errors.
- Presentation format is consistent.

It is important that QA takes the time to test an application similarly to how a client may use the application. QA should confirm the following:

- The application is easy to follow.
- Information is straightforward, informative, and appropriate.
- Fields that need to be filled in are checked to make sure they accept correct information and reject incorrect information.
- Pictures, illustrations, and movies run correctly and provide appropriate content.
- Help screens are easy to access and informative.
- Information gathered is updated correctly.
- Access screens or password protection works.

The role of the people developing the application and the web editors during the QA phase is to support the QA organization and to fix bugs in a timely manner. Near the end of QA, the programmers or web editor should create and present a class explaining how the site or application works. The audience of this class is the help desk or client support organization and any other employees involved in supporting the project through the beta process. The purpose of this class is for technical project information to be transferred from the programmers or web editor to the support organization. The class is referred to as a *transfer of information* (TOI). The help desk representative works with the programming representative to the team to make sure that the information programming presents meets the needs of the support organization. The help desk representative is responsible for inviting the appropriate people within their organization.

During the QA phase the documentation writer reviews changes and recommendations provided by QA. The documentation writer incorporates these changes. During the QA phase the writer may augment the documents by creating install, usage, and debug samples. It is important that QA presents to the team each week their test status and an annotated bug count. Once QA certifies that they have run all their tests and there are no severity-1 or severity-2 bugs, the project can move to the next level of testing, beta.

Beta

After QA tests the product, the product is given to a select group of clients who also test it. This client test period is referred to as beta. Members from the team are selected; their responsibility is to develop the beta plan and client beta questionnaire. The beta period takes place after the QA phase is complete. During the QA phase, the QA organization tests the product and confirms that the product meets the specifications outlined in the requirements document and design document and confirms that the documentation developed by the writer is adequate and meets the requirements specified in the documentation plan. After QA declares the product acceptable to enter beta, the product is sent to a selected group of clients who test and confirm that the product works as specified. Beta is an extension of quality assurance. Beta provides quality testing by allowing clients to confirm that the product meets their specifications in a nonlab environment. The team needs to agree what the beta period should look like. An example of a beta period specification created by a product team is as follows: It will be necessary to beta-test this product at a minimum of five sites to a maximum of fifteen sites over a fifteen-day beta cycle.

For a company that has an existing intranet and is adding a new application, an e-mail might be sent to a selected group of clients asking the clients to beta-test the site. The clients will receive an e-mail identifying the following:

- The application's scope and purpose
- What is being requested of the people testing the application

- Any special information the client will need in order to run the program (special codes, passwords)
- URL to access the application
- Comment sheet for e-mail feedback

Note: It may be prudent to send the e-mail to employees, allowing them to test the site even if the application is for the Internet. It may be difficult to control and explain the "beta" nature of the test to intranet clients. If the application is for customers, allowing sales to beta-test the application can be a first step in acceptance. If sales visits the site and navigates through the screens, they will feel more comfortable explaining this new business procedure to customers. For an intranet, a new application can be made available to a specific department. Once QA can verify that the department used the application and the application ran smoothly, the application can be rolled out to a larger group of people.

QA and a team member who works closely with the client (help desk for an intranet, marketing for an Internet) need to define a beta plan. The beta plan consists of a list of action items that will ensure a successful beta, identifying who in the company is responsible for the action items and assigning a begin and end date to ensure that the beta will begin and end on time. Depending on the scope of the application, not all information outlined below may be needed. A sample of items that may be covered in a beta plan follows:

Tasks	Group
- Identify potential beta sites	Marketing/Help Desk/Sales
- Decide minimum configuration and features to be tested	QA/Programming

- Draft beta questionnaire
  a. Client information
  b. Site environment information
	Marketing and QA

- Prepare check list of technologies to be tested	QA
- Fill in beta questionnaire for each potential site	Marketing/Help Desk

- Bring beta site information to
  product team   Marketing/Help Desk
- Prepare beta contract   Legal
- Set up install date with client   Marketing/Help Desk/QA
- Establish beta committee   QA
- Prepare beta site test plan   QA
- Prepare beta site cover letter   Marketing
- Ship product   QA
- Monitor beta progress   Help Desk or QA
- Ship or e-mail beta updates   Help Desk or QA
- Beta sign-off call and sheet (re-
  view tested features)   QA
- Review and send sign-off sheet
  and approve sign-off   Team
- Prepare beta sign-off letter   Marketing/Help Desk
- Send beta site a gift   Marketing/Help Desk

The Beta Questionnaire

For larger intranet applications or client applications it may be
necessary to have a more formal procedure for beta-testing a
new application than sending an e-mail with a URL. A document might need to be created and reviewed with potential beta
clients to confirm that their site meets the needs of the product,
that the site is qualified and interested in testing the product,
and that the team has the necessary information on each beta
site. Examples of questions asked in a beta questionnaire appear
below.

Information Necessary to Qualify a Potential Beta Site

- Company name and address, along with the key contact
  name, phone number, fax number, and e-mail address
- System configuration(s) and operating system release
  level

Potential beta sites may be considered once the following
information has been verified:

- The beta machine must have (minimum hardware configuration).
- The beta client must have (minimum software configuration) prior to the beta.
- The beta client understands that problems with a beta product may interrupt normal operations. We therefore request that the beta take place in a noncritical production environment.
- The beta client must provide status updates to (company name) (beta coordinator name) on a weekly basis.
- The beta client must complete the beta evaluation questionnaire after the beta is over.
- The beta client must commit to beta-testing this product for a minimum of XX days.
- The beta client will be provided with preliminary documentation, which may be incomplete or contain errors. If the client elects to purchase the product, this documentation will be replaced.

Identifying Beta Sites

For Internet applications, marketing needs to work closely with sales to identify clients who would be good prospective beta sites. Finding good beta sites is probably one of the most difficult tasks of the beta program. Many customers do not have the facilities or time to test a project properly. Most clients who are interested in testing a new application want the functionality of the application so they can work more efficiently. This can cause potential problems, since live sites usually cannot tolerate errors. It is very important to impress upon clients that this code is beta quality. That means that it has been tested internally but not tested in a live environment, and that there is a high probability that there will be bugs.

Once marketing identifies potential beta sites, it is necessary to interview these sites and confirm that they can and will test the application during the assigned beta period. The beta questionnaire is reviewed with the client. Marketing should check again to make sure that the potential beta sites are agreeable at launch time.

One recommendation for a successful beta is to sign up twice as many sites as the team specified, since there is a high probability that up to half of the committed beta sites will not be able to test the project during the allotted time. It is wise to remember that beta sites are doing the company a favor. Treat them accordingly. If a good relationship is developed with a beta site, then the next time a project is to enter beta, the site is usually willing to be a participant.

Pricing

You might decide that your site or application should be accessed for a fee. Hopefully you decided this up front and have designed in password protection that can be given to people who purchase your services. Pricing is a strong competitive weapon. Many web sites are offering free access to entice people to visit their site. They hope once consumers become hooked they can then begin charging for their site or add additional fee services. Currently the web is like an interactive cable TV. Clients will pay for products but are not yet ready to pay for access. Another approach is to charge advertising fees for other companies to advertise their site on your site. Companies can place banners and pointers on your site. As with print advertising, companies will pay based on visibility and demographics. To have paid advertising you will need to provide hit rates and demographics for your site. Be careful when pricing a site. Flame mail is quick and noisy on the Internet. You don't want to make a big splash that will cause a negative outcry. Read Internet trade magazines, follow trends, and make sure you are making an informed decision when pricing a web site or web application.

If you decide to price an Internet service, you should have begun to identify price/cost in your requirements document created in Chapter 3. Pricing is set in accordance with the corporation's competitive positioning. For instance, if the company is selling a service against a market leader, they may set the price of their service at fifteen percent below the competitor's price. It is necessary for marketing to understand how price is used in the sales process and what pricing situations the sales force needs to overcome with price. For example, if you are selling a service that has more features than the industry leader, but the client makes their decision on price, you can create a core product that meets the functionality of the industry leader and charge less than the industry leader. Then you can create add-on modules, for an additional price, for your added functionality. This will provide the client with a direct comparison and highlight your additional functionality. The pieces of information management needs from marketing when creating a pricing plan are:

- Project list price
- Assumed discount for large customers
- Competitive pricing
- Dollar and percentage difference between competitor and project

For an existing project, executives need to know

- If the price will change
- The dollar and percentage change proposed
- The effect this change will have on the company's projected revenue

If the service is to be sold internationally, this information needs to be provided for each country, along with the sales price equivalent in U.S. dollars and difference in dollar percentage. (A company sells the product for $20 in Europe, $15 in the U.S. The dollar difference is $5; the percentage difference is twenty-five percent.) The Internet provides a level playing field. Traditionally American companies have charged more internationally for the same service or products. Internet applications have changed this model. Since everyone has equal access and most services are purchased by credit card, international exchange issues and price differentials rarely exist.

By the end of development and beta you should have created and fully tested your site and application and feel very comfortable that the site is functioning. It is better to push back the availability date of an application or site than to put a site up that is not working correctly. Once you feel confident about your site, you can publish your content or application. This is a celebration opportunity. Plan a party, and have all the people associated with your new site or application invited. Spend some time enjoying the fact that you completed your project.

7

Marketing Your Internet/Intranet Site

Marketing an Internet site is very different from marketing an intranet site. This chapter is broken into two sections: Internet marketing and intranet marketing.

Internet Marketing

Defining Your Launch Goals

Earlier you should have decided on the goal and benefit of your site. This goal should have been your central theme when creating web content and working with your design firm. When marketing your site it is important that you stay true to your goal. If you decided that your goal was to provide company or product information to established customers and the benefit of this goal was to increase customer satisfaction, your entire marketing campaign should be focused on these issues. Companies have been know to change themes in the eleventh hour. Someone within the company will decide that a different goal is "sexier" than their intended goal. The thrust of their marketing campaign will be on this new goal. Companies that change their campaign in the eleventh hour usually have failed campaigns. The message and the content need to match. The responsibility of a launch is to highlight the accomplishment. Stay true to your goal and you will have a successful launch.

Some companies silently launch a web site. Launch size and scope should be based on what you want to accomplish with your web site and the budget you have to create your launch. The minimum requirements in launching a web site are as follows:

- Add web site locators to collateral as new collateral is printed.
- Educate employees on the scope and purpose of the web site.
- Contact locator sites to add your URL and description to their search criteria.
- Send a press release to the business wire.

Depending on the purpose of your site, you may want to create a full-blown launch.

Creating a Launch Plan for an Internet Site

For an Internet launch, marketing should be involved from the beginning in creating a launch plan. Typically it will take three or four months before the site goes live to create a successful launch. A launch plan details how, when, and who will be responsible for developing each deliverable needed to successfully launch a web site. Part of the launch plan is to create a budget for the project and receive budget approval. This should be done outside of the team, with the team informed when the budget is approved. If this is an international project, extra care needs to be taken when developing the strategy and identifying the time frames. Translations need to be made for each country's language and culture. If the launch is to be simultaneously occurring, worldwide schedules need to be built that allow time for localization. An effective American campaign does not always play well in Europe. It needs to be decided if materials that are developed will be deployed around the world or if new materials will be developed for each market. Budget, politics, and client demographics play into this decision.

Launch Strategy

When launching your product, think strategically. What is the company's long-range goal, and how will an Internet site fit into this goal? A good marketing organization has created a long-range (two-year) introduction and launch advertising strategy. This strategy articulates how the company is going to use new announcements, advertisements, press releases, magazine articles and speaking engagements to build on itself and create momentum in developing an image, market direction, or market share. Make sure your Internet site is included in this long-range plan. The site's announcement can be used as one step in the strategy. After the site goes on-line, it can be used to magnify the momentum of the strategy. Highly visited web sites are a great advertisement vehicle.

Positioning Your Story

Launches are stories. To be successful when launching a web site you will need to create a compelling story. It's marketing's responsibility to create a story around your company's goals. The story needs to be sympathetic to the listener. Decide who your audience is and create a story that focuses on the needs of the listener. The story must always stay true to the goal of the web site. A company that has a unique product line might launch a web site as a means of providing access to their unique product to a larger audience. When the company pitches their web site to the investment community, they should focus on the ability of the Internet to access a larger market. The financial community is interested in the company's revenue generation. When pitching the story to a magazine that is read by potential customers, the company focuses on how easy it will be for people interested in these unique products to learn more about the products, and how clients can easily visit the site, view the products, and get product and pricing information. Both stories are true to the goal of the site while being sympathetic to the needs of the audience.

It is marketing's responsibility to be intimately familiar with the client, the competition, industry, press, and analysts.

Marketing usually relies on a public relations (PR) firm to assist them in keeping up on the latest themes with press and analysts. Good public relations people have ongoing relationships with press and analysts and can assist marketing in focusing the story. The marketing and PR teams should know how to focus the story to meet the needs of the audience. Within an audience there are themes. The press goes through phases looking for stories that meet certain objectives. Marketing and PR are responsible for having a tight pulse on the current themes the press is writing about. PR should recommend the best way to present the site verbally and visually. A theme for a cycling magazine might be nutrition for long rides. A vitamin company that is putting up a new web site in order to reach a broader market might get featured in an article if they pitch their story based on their nutrition chat line.

Marketing is responsible for managing the launch process. Launch deliverables may come from many people, both internal and external to the company. Marketing needs to decide how, where, and when it is best to launch the site. Depending on the site and the visibility of the company, it may be wise to announce the site in conjunction with a major trade show or product announcement. Depending on the size of the company or the uniqueness of the site, some announcements obtain better visibility when released during slack news periods. Considerations that affect the announcement date may be competitive launches and newsworthy subjects that can gain better visibility for the site. For example, a bank developing an Internet banking solution might want to announce their web site in conjunction with an article in a major magazine highlighting how the Internet is changing the way people bank. They can increase visibility by being featured in this article. Depending on who your target audience is, it might be worthwhile to get featured in a technology magazine. If you solved an interesting business problem and have a nicely articulated site, a technology vendor might want to spotlight your site. A vendor with a popular site can increase your site's traffic flow by including a pointer to your site from the spotlight in the vendor's site.

Companies should be careful not to introduce a site too soon. A competitor's announcement may drive a company to feel they need to introduce a web site or new application early. This approach can backfire. Press and analysts take into account release dates and referenced beta sites for web applications. When release dates are far out for an application and beta sites cannot be identified by the press, analysts notice and highlight the immaturity of the launch. If the site is not complete, graphics are unprofessional, users get led to blind alleys, help screens have not been incorporated, or the application runs slowly, a reporter might write about these drawbacks. Customers might shy away from using the application or visiting the site either by reading bad press on the site or by visiting an incomplete or uninteresting site.

Companies should choose their launch date based on what will gain them the most positive press. It is unwise to lose the momentum of a launch by being viewed as a "me too" announcement. Give the competitor time to deliver. Many times competitors launch an application or web site early in order to receive early press. They want to be the first with an Internet solution. If the project release date slips or the site's quality is poor or uninteresting, an advantage can be made when releasing your solution. The best strategy to take when a competitor releases a new site is to show sportsmanlike conduct. A countermeasure is to entice the press by *overhanging the market*. Overhanging the market is a strategy whereby you entice the press to speculate about a soon-to-be released project by trickling out information. For instance, a company is due to announce a breakthrough Internet solution in six months; their competitor announces a solution today. The company with the breakthrough technology tells the media that they are not concerned about this new announcement, since they will be announcing a breakthrough solution in six months. The press will then begin to speculate about this breakthrough technology. Clients will hold off on purchasing the newly announced solution, waiting for the breakthrough solution. This plan can backfire if the breakthrough is not a breakthrough. Also, since the press is wise to overhanging the market, you will need to give them a nondisclosure presentation of what you are planning to announce in order for them to help you overhang the market.

Creating a Launch Plan

The eight areas to be considered in a launch plan are: message development, press kit development, contacting analysts and journalists, announcement date, collateral, web and trade advertising, joint site coordination, and Internet registration.

1. *Message development.* It is the responsibility of the corporate officers to provide corporate direction and the corporate message. It is the responsibility of marketing to take this message and direction and articulate it. Marketing provides positioning and demographic information so that a positioning statement can be developed by public relations that will properly target the client. The message was begun when the product was approved. Use the goal and benefit developed in Chapter 3 as the basis of your message development. Make sure you focus your message on the benefit of the target audience. You should have identified who your target audience is in Chapter 3. If you are presenting your new site to the financial community, you may want to highlight cost savings or revenue generation. If you are presenting your message to clients, you may want to highlight speed, ease of use, and convenience. The site and corporate messages are the fundamental idea behind a site release. It is necessary for the corporate message to incorporate the site message and for each to be in concert with the other. The company's market position needs to be taken into account when releasing a new site or application. Before a release, any updates to corporate positioning should be made. Corporate positioning explains to the outside world who the company is and how it views itself. The corporate presentation defines the company's target market and the position it has within the market. Positioning explains what the Internet application or site is, who will access the site, why they need it, and why the company is offering a site.

2. *Press kit development.* After the project and corporate positioning is complete, the press kit deliverables can be developed. The project was defined in the requirements document. Marketing can use this definition as a basis for defining the site.

The following is a list of items that should be included in a press kit:

- Press release—Marketing writes a press release based on the site goals and site definition. The press release is modified for the business wire.
- Case studies—Marketing interviews beta clients and documents these interviews in case studies. Case studies can be given to the press and your sales organization as examples of how the site solves client needs.
- Corporate backgrounder—The corporate backgrounder augments the corporate presentation. It is a high-level document presenting the company, corporate officers, financial status, target market, market share, and short- and long-range corporate goals.
- Executive backgrounder—This refers to information sheets introducing the executive team. One to two paragraphs review the executive's past jobs and educational history.
- Corporate and site positioning statement—Highlights of the company's goals, where it sees itself fitting in to its industry, and the direction the company is moving in should be summarized. The site or application should then be presented as one step in the process of the company's meeting its goal. The corporate and project positioning is edited to meet the needs of press and analysts.
- Data sheets—If applicable, data sheets on the site or the application accessed through the site are created.

All of this information is put in a folder. Journalists, upon returning to their office, now have a complete background on what the company is, the company's goals and objectives, the people who make up the executive team, and the detail on the site or new service. When the journalist writes his article, he has the details he may need in one place.

3. *Contacting analysts and journalists.* Marketing works with the PR firm to create a list of analysts that influence the target clients. PR is responsible for identifying the correct analyst, checking if any upcoming analyst reports are applicable to your launch, reviewing the reports for impact, and developing a strategy of how best to update the analysts. Analysts are the most

influential of the media, and special time needs to be taken to make sure the analysts are briefed early so that their comments can be incorporated into the overall message.

The client demographic information is used to identify which media should be pitched to. Marketing works with PR to identify the themes that need to be developed for pitching the stories. The correct writer and correct positioning for each publication needs to be identified. Marketing needs to identify if certain analysts and press will receive the information early or if they will receive the information during the press tour. Considerations are made due to press dates since some publications need a longer lead time. If a magazine or writer has been supportive of the company, marketing may decide to give that writer an early scoop.

4. *Announcement date.* If applicable, an appropriate date to announce the project needs to be decided. Before the announcement date, the press release needs to be mailed to the press with whom the company has set up appointments. If the site is a large corporate announcement and the company is introducing interesting new Internet tools, an East Coast, West Coast, European, and Asian press tour needs to be defined and appointments scheduled. This is where monthlies, weeklies, and dailies are pitched the site story. A good PR firm is instrumental in assisting in this process. The PR firm will help identify the press and analysts, know upcoming stories that may fit, set the schedule for the press tour, and review the handouts to make sure they are clear and targeted.

5. *Collateral.* The deliverables available to the sales force and clients need to be modified to answer their needs. Slides and scripts need to modified or added to current corporate presentations to include pertinent information about the WWW site. If the site has secure access or special pricing options, the information needs to be articulated to the field. Current data sheets need to include the WWW address. You should surf the Internet and be aware of how your site compares to other sites, especially those in your industry. The corporate positioning and site positioning need to be articulated to the sales force and clients. Training needs to be coordinated with the sales organization so

the site or application and information on how to position these new resources to customers can be explained to the sales channel. Sales should get a preview of the site, giving them time to become familiar with the screens and understand how the company is going to market and use the site.

6. *Web and trade advertising.* This area includes the following:

Traditional media: After the project is released, appropriate advertising needs to be created. The client demographic information is used to determine the most effective advertising campaign. Magazine ads, direct mail, and telemarketing campaigns need to be designed and coordinated. The web site's goal is the central theme in creating the advertising. For example, the local water utility company might want to create a campaign that runs on local TV and in the daily newspaper. The goal of this campaign is to get people familiar with the site and increase site traffic. The site's goal is to make the utility appear to be a valued member of the community. If the region is experiencing a drought, TV and news spots might ask consumers to be water-wise gardeners. The ads can entice clients to visit the site to learn more on how to be water-wise gardeners. Water bills would include an advertisement enticing customers to visit the web site. The insert may include a tip on water-wise gardening, the web site address, and a few words explaining why customers should visit the site. The web site could spotlight water-wise gardening. The site could include hints on maintaining gardens with little water, resource listings including drought-resistant plants and irrigation systems, and tips for water-wise gardening. Gardening chat lines and articles written by local gardening experts could round out the site. By featuring timely content, the site becomes a destination location and the utility can foster an image of community involvement and concern.

Internet: The Internet also has advertising. Popular sites let you buy banners that can link to your site. Like other media, information is available on site demographics and hit numbers. Internet demographics tend to be sketchy since it is an immature media. The media buyer at your advertising agency might have information on Internet site advertising. If not, get on-line and search on Internet advertising. Sites that sell advertising usually have a section on their demographics and hit rates.

7. *Joint site coordination.* Another way to increase web attendance is by sharing pointers to other sites. If you are part of a trade organization, you can request a pointer to your site in other members' sites. Most sites want you to reciprocate the service. Get on the web and use a search engine to identify sites that would be symbiotic or share similar client demographics. Send an e-mail to the site's web master asking for a reciprocal link. You will need to create a compelling reason why he should link to your site. Most likely he will surf your site, confirming that the information in your site is appropriate.

8. *Internet registration.* When you go live you will need to register your site with the major search engines (Yahoo, Alta-Vista, . . .) so that potential clients can find you. You can go to each search engine's home page to register. Usually there is an icon to register your URL location. All sites will want your URL. Sometimes the search engine will want information on your site: this might include a twenty-five-word-or-less explanation of your site. Other sites might want you to register your site using their criteria system. The site will take you through the steps necessary to get registered. There are also free registration services. To find one of these services, search on "Internet site registration." You will get a listing of sites that help you register. Registration sites will take your information and pass it to many other sites.

Marketing a web site is an ongoing process. Once you have done the initial marketing and recognition, you will need to decide what you want to achieve with a web site. If you are looking at creating a destination location, you will need to continue to change web content. You will need to create events that cause clients to want to bookmark and visit your site. Marketing of a web site will remain dynamic. The best plan is to use your web site as one element in all marketing activities. Your advertisements should reference your WWW location. Your web site should be coordinated with your advertising campaigns. You can use your web site as one means of disseminating information. Publish press releases, and create pointers to positive articles written on your company or products. Use your web site as an effective tool for supporting clients.

Selling an Internet Tool

You will need to market your Internet tools. An example of an Internet tool is found in Chapter 4, business case 3, where a manufacturing company created an Internet ordering tool for its customers. The type of tool and target client will dictate what type of marketing campaign you will need to create. A tool like the one discussed in business case 3 will need to be coordinated with your sales organization. You should include sales and customer support in your beta process; they will need to be trained on the application. You will need to explain to them the change in procedures this tool will create. You will need to provide customer-oriented benefits along with the benefits this new tool will create for them. Don't get caught up in the technology. Don't give sales and support more information than they need. Give the salespeople the beta URL, and let them sign on to the beta site and try out the application. Listen to the sales feedback. They know the customer; they will give you good information. Filter this information with the fact that this application represents a change in procedures for them. Change also leads to skepticism and fear. Be sympathetic to their concern for change.

Next you will need to create a campaign to notify customers of this site and service. Make sure the sales and support people are notified of this customer campaign. Provide sales and support with samples of the literature customers will be receiving. You may include a brochure announcing your new site in the information your company regularly sends to your customers. You might want to send a brochure directly to the person who would use the site. If you collect e-mail addresses from customers, you should send an e-mail to targeted customers explaining the new service and providing the URL. If your salespeople make on-site visits you can train the salespeople to show the customer how to sign on to the service. Train the salespeople to bookmark customers' browsers. Sites that are targeted at general customers will need a more general awareness campaign. A general application might be a package application (Federal Express, UPS). Include information on your site in your sales literature and ad campaigns. Train your service representatives to remind customers they can check packages on-line if they have an Internet connection. Create a simple insert explaining the service and providing the URL. Include this insert in all packages and mailings. As long as the application exists you should market your site. After first launch you might want to make sure all brochures have a note explaining how you can track packages through the WWW.

Intranet Site Marketing

Selling an intranet internally is very different from marketing an Internet site. The goal of selling an intranet site or application is to get your company using the site as a central communication tool. A successful plan should focus on educating fellow employees on how this tool will help them to do their job better. A good plan of action is to break the intranet internal sales process into easily digested parts:

1. Get executive support.
2. Get the word out.
3. Make people feel comfortable using this tool.
4. Teach employees how to augment the site by adding their own content.

Get Executive Support

The most effective intranets are those used by executive staff. Employees will use the intranet if their boss uses it. Start at the top; take the time to teach the CEO and senior-level executives how to use the site. If you get the senior-level people using e-mail, the whole company will get on e-mail very quickly. If the CEO comments on a good web page or helpful utility, the news will spread. You can leverage executive buy-in for the project you received up front with commitment to use the technology now. Explain to the executives how important it is to the company to use this technology. Focus the benefits of using the technology on executives' needs: fast way to communicate, good way for them to keep their pulse on the company and keep corporate communication active while traveling. Don't focus on the technology; they don't have to know how this thing works. Load the executives' PCs with the web browser before you train them. Test and make sure the connection is working. Have them sign on to the intranet, have them navigate through the applications, have them send their direct reports on e-mail. Go back in a few days, and make sure they respond to e-mails sent. Have a short, informal e-mail drafted that they can send to their organization. Have this e-mail state how excited they are that they have this new tool for communication and, that they expect employees will use this new tool. You may have them include the e-mail policy you created earlier.

Establish Awareness

The next goal is to make employees aware that the site or application is available. Effective awareness campaigns focus on the benefits to the employees. Don't be condescending. Understand that change causes resistance. The resistance can be expressed in a number of ways. Some employees act skeptically; others will view the new tool as the latest toy; still others might complain that this is one more thing added to their already overburdened workload. Focus on the benefit; listen to the resistance. Don't overcome the objections. Repeat the listeners' concerns, and be sympathetic. For instance, if an employee says it's just one more thing to do, you can reply, "I understand you are concerned about your workload." The employee will feel respected, and his resistance to learn will be lowered.

Depending on your budget and your corporate culture, there are many ways you can advertise your site internally:

- Have the site's availability mentioned in staff meetings.
- Have the site featured in a company magazine.
- Place a banner in the cafeteria.
- Have a message broadcast to all employees using the existing computer infrastructure.
- Put a flyer in employees' mail folder.

Make Employees Feel Comfortable Through Training and Education

Education will be dependent on company size and the location of employees. For a single-location company, a member of the IS staff can visit departmental meetings and present the site. Don't focus on the technology or the audience will be lost. Train employees to use a browser. Show them where to place a URL and how to bookmark locations. Preconfigure the browser so the company's home page is automatically displayed. Show employees how to navigate through the available services. Have a handout of the home page and the browser. Have this picture annotated with key interest zones (URL, bookmark, e-mail). The writer deployed in Chapter 5 may have created an introductory document explaining the intranet site. This is a good time to pass out this document. The document should list the services employees can access from the intranet site. Don't get technical; employees don't need to know how it works.

Get the people in the group to gather around a computer (you can bring a portable). Show the group how easy it is to log on and find information. Choose one person in the group; the most timid person would be good. Be very patient; have this person perform a simple task—find his name in the phone book, look up HR policies. Have a few other people try it out. A good training session is interactive. Keep the group small, and let them do the demo. For companies that have offices located throughout a large region, get on the agenda for any remote headquarter training. The people in the class can be your good-will ambassadors. The reason companies are using Internet technology for their intranet is because this technology is easy to learn and simple to work with. Training should be short and simple. Take the time to explain company policies. You can set up a training booth in the cafeteria, and employees can stop by to learn about the intranet. If you budgeted for it, you can give away coffee mugs or T-shirts to employees who get trained.

Show Your Employees How to Augment the System Through Page Creation

As your intranet grows, groups will want to put their information on the company's web. There are applications available that create html documents using a desktop publishing interface. The application allows employees to create html documents without having to know html. Employees should not need to take a class in html programming. It might be worthwhile for your company to bring in an instructor who can periodically give a half-day class in web creation. Everyone attending the class can be given the company's guidelines for web creation and be shown where they can find the web templates and available illustrations. The instructor can hit the highlights about laying out usable pages and explain how to publish a created page.

The web master should provide departmental managers with the location and password for publishing information in their section of the company's site. The departmental manager can decide how information gets published for his department. The web master should provide the departmental manager with guidelines, such as the following:

- Use the established corporate style guide.
- Be grammatically correct.
- Have material appropriate for viewing by the entire company.
- If access to the information is limited, place the information behind a password protection, or give the URL limited-access restrictions.
- Make sure all information is legal (will not compromise the company).

Now that employees know how to access the site and are using the intranet, you can start the whole process over again by implementing new features. New features are much easier to train employees on. With an existing intranet you can advertise the new intranet feature on the corporate home page, providing pointers and on-line education. An e-mail message can be sent to everyone in the company highlighting the features of the new site and providing the new feature's URL. A banner can be placed in the cafeteria announcing the new feature. Each time you create a new application or series of applications you will need to start this process over again. Don't shortcut the process.

Figure 7-1. Release Cycle

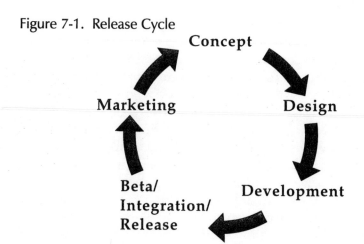

You can reuse elements created previously. Make sure you keep yourself and your team focused by taking the time to create a concept plan, business case, design document, development, QA beta, and product rollout.

8

Managing a Site

Once a site has been created, it now needs to be managed and maintained so that it can continue to provide timely, accurate information.

Managing an Intranet

An intranet web master and web editor will strive to make the corporate intranet a destination location that provides utilities, tools, and information to make employees efficient and effective. If employees are frustrated navigating through their intranet web site, the web master and web editor will receive a lot of flak. Spending the time up front to design a workable site has many long-term paybacks.

Many companies and organizations have a decentralized intranet. The web master maintains the intranet technology infrastructure, while the web editor lays out the corporate design criteria and flow. Each department can decide if they want to create their own intranet web site. If a department wants to add their own departmental site to the corporate intranet, they will need to approach the web editor and ask to be included in the corporate web site. It is important that a company has a central person responsible for managing intranet sites. Without a central web editor, employees may spend too much time attempting to find intranet destinations. With central management the web editor can lay out easy access paths for departmental sites. A well-organized web editor will have already planned for the growth of the intranet by laying out clear paths for each department and creating a training class or packet of information explaining corporate policies, procedures, and guidelines to create an effective web site.

Once a department decides they want a web site, they can request IS to develop an application that will help them manage corporate duties. For example, the marketing organization might have the responsibility for company giveaways. Giveaways may include shirts, coffee cups, or pens. An organization wanting a giveaway can access the marketing site and fill in a simple on-line giveaway form. Marketing can include pictures of giveaways already created on their giveaway page. After an employee fills out the form, marketing can have an approval form automatically generated. Putting this information on-line will create easier fulfillment and management control. The facilities department might decide to include an on-line request page within their site. If an employee has a facilities problem, like a broken bookshelf or a light that has gone out, the employee can access the facilities site, enter in the problem, and identify its location. This will make it easier for facilities to log, manage, and fulfill employee requests.

The web editor and web master will need to work closely together to coordinate applications and the extended sites within a company. As the sites become decentralized, departments will start using their site for more than on-line forms access. Departmental managers will see the benefit of spotlighting their group's functions, highlighting accomplishments, and providing corporate insight into their group's functions. For example, a research department might want to include its corporate charter, technology breakthroughs, and awards. A chief engineer can discuss his philosophy and goals. Employees within a department can create personal web pages highlighting their personal interests or professional accomplishments. An intranet can be used by employees to put a human face on their organization. As departments begin to explore the use of a departmental web site, a web editor will need to assist this exploration with good, solid design recommendations and guidelines. There are a few types of guidelines the web editor will need to create.

Figure 8-1. Example of an Employee Home Page

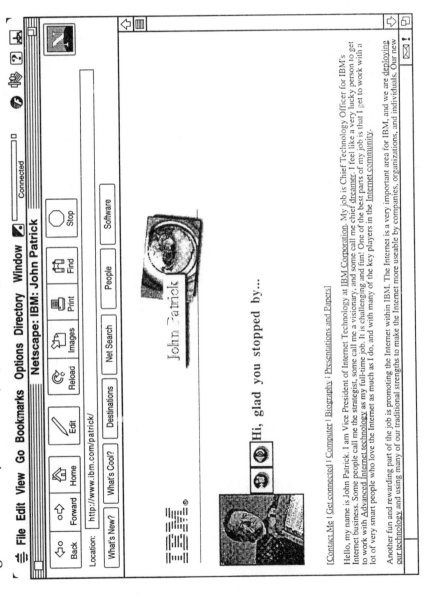

Personal web page guidelines. A company should create guidelines before employees begin creating personal web pages. Examples of acceptable web pages should be created so employees have a starting point. Much of the information on personal web pages depends on corporate culture. Some companies enjoy having employees include pictures of their dogs or kids, while other companies prefer employees to keep web pages focused on work-related activities. There are some good, easy-to-use tools available for people to develop their personal web page. Netscape and Microsoft each include a personal web page creator with their browser.

Confidential information guidelines. Many departments create confidential information. Guidelines should be created so that employees are aware what information is confidential and what information is repeatable. A good rule of thumb is that information that is for internal use only, information that can be viewed by any employee, can be put on the web page. Restricted information, information that should not have corporate access, should not be accessible by everyone. Departments can work with the web editor to create password-protected sites. This is beneficial so that restricted information can be shared via a web site by people with access. Many times confidential information needs to be shared between employees within a group or between groups. Placing confidential information behind a security password within the corporate intranet ensures that need-to-know employees have access to the latest version. For example, a company might be in the process of creating a new competitive product. They have created a design document for this product. Specific employees within product development, quality assurance, and manufacturing need access to this design document. Employees outside of the project team do not need access. By putting the design document on the intranet with password protection, employees with permission can check the latest version of the document.

The web master should create a background template for internal use only and for confidential information. Departments creating confidential information and placing this information on their web site can use the appropriate background template.

Employees viewing or printing the information will instantly recognize the internal nature of this information. An example might be a department's organization chart. A department might want their organization chart accessible by everyone in the company, but they might not want it given to people outside of the company, since they are concerned that headhunters may be targeting their employees. The organization chart can be viewed by anyone within the company. The background of the organization chart will read *Internal use only*.

Legal guidelines. Legal guidelines will stop potential lawsuits before they happen and create a legal due-diligence audit trail. The web editor should work with the company's lawyer to draft a list of items that can be potential legal problems for the company. The most obvious items that would cause legal problems are items that are politically incorrect such as sexually explicit, religious, or ethnic slurs. Recently a large company was involved in a class-action sexual discrimination lawsuit. The plaintiff's lawyers searched out items that would show that the company fostered an atmosphere of sexual discrimination. One item used as an example was an e-mail *spam* (e-mail message sent to a wide distribution list). The e-mail was titled "Why beer is better than women." The e-mail contained sexually rude material. This company currently has a very stringent policy regarding e-mail humor. They have been known to have employees who break the "humor spam" rule to send an apology to all recipients of the offensive humor.

Due to the dynamic nature of an intranet, not every web page or every e-mail message can be controlled. If employees are provided with a clear understanding of what is acceptable and what is unacceptable, potential problems will be curtailed before they happen. The company should also set a policy clearly stating what will happen to employees who break the legal guidelines. This may range from automatic deletion of the web page to a formal reprimand. The web editor should work with the human resources EEOC coordinator to make sure intranet guidelines are included in their training materials.

Management guidelines. Departments creating a web site should appoint their own departmental web editor. It is easiest for a department to create an internal web site if there is one person in control of the department's web site. The company web master can create a web editor training class. This class can show a departmental web editor how to lay out a web site, create simple html documents, review company policies, highlight effective ways to create web copy, and detail how to work with IS to create departmental applications. The departmental web editor can be the central point of contact for the web editor and web master.

Components That Make Up a Good Internet/Intranet Site

Throughout the book we have discussed the components of an Internet/intranet site. Once the site has been created and is working, it is necessary to keep the site current and decide if new applications are in order. The new components should augment or clarify the existing site. It is important to make sure new components meet a basic set of standards. The same design criteria will be necessary to reach clients outside of an organization as within an organization.

The eight basic components of a good Internet/intranet site are:

1. *Use first-person narrative.* When clients visits your sites, it is as if they are getting a personal tour of your company or department. You wouldn't take a potential customer, business partner, or employee on a tour and refer to your company as "them." Likewise, you wouldn't overwhelm the person on the tour with talk and never show them what they came looking for. A good way to write site copy is to use first-person narrative and not overwhelm the client with lots of words. When possible, break thoughts into bulleted items. Provide illustrations to highlight your point.

2. *Write using clear, simple language.* Your site will be accessed by many people with varying degrees of knowledge. The sites home page should use simple, clear words and terminol-

ogy. The rule of thumb is to write at a fourth-grade level. Remember, your site will be visited by people who are not native English speakers or are not experts in your field. For example, an engineer might want to include his "straw man" proposal on his department's intranet. It is recommended that he include an executive overview that uses nontechnical terminology. The technical document can follow. The engineer should make it clear that the technical document uses technical terminology. By clearly identifying the nature of documents you will avoid overwhelming or frustrating clients by a site. Another example is the company's legal department. The legal department might want to have a site that includes the company's legal position concerning a recent lawsuit. The actual legal document might follow a layman's explanation of the proceedings.

3. *Clearly state your site's goal.* The first page of your site should have enough information on your company or department that a client entering your site knows that he has reached his intended destination. Either give a brief description of your company, department, or products or provide an easily accessible section that explains your company, department, or product. For example, a research department with an intranet web site might want to have the first page provide a summary of the department's goal. After a one- or two-sentence overview, the page might reference places the client can visit: (1) products currently in design, (2) group achievements, (3) design philosophy, (4) people within the group.

4. *Make it clear what the site's goal is.* Don't provide a section on customer support that can't support a client. A client visiting a customer support site that only explains the goals of your customer support organization without providing a FAQ or a place to ask questions will leave your site frustrated and dismayed. If you don't have the infrastructure to support an application the right way, tell the client visiting your site that the service is under construction and give them an approximate time they can expect the site to be functioning. It is better not to include a nonfunctioning site than to provide a path but no real content.

5. *Give clients a place to go.* Don't create an informational site but provide no place to ask a question. By finding only "bro-

chures on-line" but no place a client can follow up, clients become disillusioned with your site. This can be worse than having no site at all. When you do provide a place clients can go to ask questions, make sure the info line is ready to respond to questions. If this is an Internet site and your company does not sell directly to the public, make sure you provide links or clearly identify where clients can go to find your product. Don't leave potential customers searching for a distribution channel.

6. *Check your site out on a variety of PCs, Macs, and workstations.* Not everyone visiting your site will have the latest high-powered workstation with a high-speed modem. For intranet sites keep in mind that employees who are traveling on business or telecommuting will be accessing this site. If it takes minutes for a client to download beautiful graphics and animated gifs (gifs are Internet-readable artwork), clients will become restless and not bother. The beautiful art is wasted. If you have a company "art gallery" that has large files that need to be downloaded, clearly state this up front. Give the client an idea how long it will take to download the file if they are using a 14.4 or 28.8 modem. Give the client an option around the large download. Options may include a version of the screen without the large illustration.

7. *Be sympathetic to the client.* If you have a site that will be visited by blind people, be careful what kinds of graphics you are using. A blind person with an audio reader will hear "graphic" and have no idea what the graphic represents. If your site is being visited by people whose native tongue is not English, use graphics and simple words to explain the site. If older people are accessing the site, do not use little characters. If people who are working in a cube are accessing the site, make sure you give them the ability to turn off any sound.

8. *Don't create a maze.* Clients have short attention spans. Not only will they opt out of your site if it takes to long to download, they will also opt out if they become lost or find it difficult too find the information they came for. Some organizations want clients to wander through their site. This is the department store approach to merchandising: to have the client walk through accessory departments to get to his destination department. This

approach backfires. If clients cannot get to their destination screen within three screens, they will leave the site very reluctant ever to return. To end the problem of the web site maze, many companies are providing good sidebar indexes that clients can click on in order to access particular information. If you have a popular application that clients continually use, recommend that the client bookmark this location. That way they don't have to search for the location every time they enter your site. Web masters can pre-bookmark intranet client browsers before they put the browser on the client's desk. Popular sites to be bookmarked might be the employee name, phone number, and e-mail listing page, or the on-line application that reserves conference rooms.

Managing Web Traffic

Now that the site is up and running, many companies and departments need to manage the new traffic coming from the web site. The first step in managing traffic is to understand how much traffic has been created. It is very simple for a web master to track how many hits a particular site gets. Departments might want to track hits so they can show the benefit of providing Internet/intranet access. A sales support department can show that each hit is equivalent to a prospect having access to the company's product information, while an HR department managing an HR intranet can show that each benefit hit is equivalent to one benefit call or question. Departments needing to answer questions might want to measure hits versus questions so they can measure the effectiveness of the site. If there are a lot of repeat questions, the department will know that they need to add content to their page. If the site includes a FAQ but clients ask the same FAQ questions via e-mail, the department will know they need to create a more effective FAQ or a different way of displaying the frequently asked questions. Once a site is created and questions are being sent to the department, it is necessary to make sure the supporting organization is ready to handle an increase in traffic and the different form in which the questions will be arriving.

Direct Response Centers

Many companies already have direct response centers within their organizations. These centers might take the form of an inbound telemarketing support center. An inbound telemarketing center is the department designed to receive customer calls regarding product questions, shipping questions, invoicing questions, general problems, or employee questions. The people in these centers are trained to help clients and provide timely responses. These centers employ a team of trained management people who measure client satisfaction, effectiveness of employees' response, and quality and timeliness of response. Good centers are always working with clients to increase quality, lower costs, and lower response time.

Internet sites are a new avenue of creating access to a company. Over the last twenty years call response centers have become ubiquitous. Clients are comfortable and familiar with using these centers, and companies have become effective in manning and managing them. A direct response center is the logical place in most companies to receive Internet/intranet responses. When creating a web site the web team should look farther down the line and understand what kinds of responses the site will generate. Instead of having a general info address, the company can create a specified address. For example, if a soap company uses its site to field customer product questions, it might specify certain categories: laundry soap questions, dishwashing soap questions, shampoo questions, beauty bar questions. That way the questions will automatically be funneled to the correct department. If the company has limited distribution channels, it might have a page that displays the current distribution channels. Clients can e-mail for a distribution channel near them. The company can reply with the closest distribution channel. It can then use this database of requests to build a business case to increase distribution channels in a specific region or use the requests as an incentive for a distributor to support its brand.

Types of Direct Response Centers

Direct response centers can be categorized as follows:

Customer support. Clients call an 800 number to ask a question. With an intranet they can access a web page that displays the FAQ (frequently asked questions) or click on an e-mail response screen. Clients expect to receive a response within twenty-four to forty-eight hours.

Sales. Clients currently call an 800 number or fax in a request. With on-line ordering the client chooses his product, provides his credit card number, and provides his shipping information. The order is fulfilled automatically. The company can automatically generate an e-mail that confirms the product ordered and provide instructions if the client wants to change or cancel the order.

General questions. Customers with questions or complaints call the company, attempting to identify who they need to speak with. With a general info e-mail address a person will need to read e-mails and send the e-mail to the appropriate employee for resolution. The company will need to create a procedure to monitor e-mail follow-up.

Financial questions. Investors wanting information on the company can access the company's finance page. The company's annual report, stock history, current selling price, and applicable articles can be displayed. Potential investors can e-mail questions to a financial representative.

How to Staff an Internet/Intranet Direct Response Center

Many of the same skills used to manage a telephone direct response center can be used to manage an Internet direct response center. The web master should be able to provide the direct response center's management team with an idea of how many hit requests are being forwarded to a specific department. A company can expect a certain amount of hits a day. Depending on the cyclical nature of their product or special promotions, hits will increase or decrease. Staffing will need to be managed to support the hits.

Internet/intranet support centers are easier to staff than traditional phone support centers. Internet people do not expect instantaneous responses. Generally it is understood that questions will receive a response within twenty-four to forty-eight hours. This will help a manager sidestep the traditional constraints of nine-to-five phone staffing by making sure there is always a backup and always phone coverage. Internet response center managers who receive a lot of requests in one day have up to forty-eight hours to respond. This gives them time to move personnel around or increase hours to handle unexpected e-mail surges.

Hiring an Internet/intranet support person also differs from hiring a phone support person. In phone support a nice, friendly speaking voice is key. Patient, unflappable personalities are treasured. In an Internet/intranet response center writing skills are key. Since the person never speaks with the support person, good phone presence is not required. Most direct response centers interview potential employees over the phone to make sure the person's phone skills are good. The same should not be done for Internet/intranet support staff. The hiring manager should perform some of the interview over e-mail. The hiring manager should look for employees who have a clear grasp of the language, including spelling, punctuation, sentence structure, and grammar. E-mail responses do not need to be long, but they do need to be clear, accurate, and easily understandable. Some people who are great on the phone are not clear writers; others who don't have the ability to work with people on the phone could be excellent Internet e-mail people. Of course, the most flexible people for staffing are those who can work on the phone or over e-mail. People that you did not consider in the past due to their verbal limitations can now be used in Internet response centers. There are deaf people with audio readers or people who have difficult-to-understand accents who might be excellent candidates for an e-mail response center.

Creating an Effective Site

It is worthwhile for a department to perform a survey to keep their pulse on the acceptance and usability of a site or application.

Intranet Polls and Questionnaires

It is much easier to keep track of the acceptance of an intranet than of an Internet, since an intranet consists of a captive audience. It is worthwhile to create a questionnaire and e-mail it to employees on a regular basis, or to create a questionnaire that employees answer after accessing an intranet application. Companies can easily track usage of sites based on the recorded hit rate. This provides an organization with the level of interest in their site. If hits decrease, the organization can question why and develop sites that keep interest high. New sites will tend to get higher traffic than old sites. Many corporate applications are cyclical. By understanding the nature of your site you can make sure there is adequate access to popular sites. For example, if the finance department is managing a site that has up-to-the-minute company stock quotes, expect constant hits or expect employees to use the stock page as their home site. When a popular site is identified, the web master can make sure this site is located on a server that has the network bandwidth to accept the quantity of hits.

Once a site is available the organization should make sure the applications are easy to use and are productive tools. Don't assume that because you like the site everyone else likes it. When polling clients, don't ask too many questions; clients become frustrated if it takes too long to get through a list of questions. Don't put a poll on every application. Choose a site, and decide what the hot topic is. Popular and unpopular sites should be targeted for polls. If your company is very large, statistically it is necessary to survey only 2,000 clients in order to get a good picture of the acceptance of a site. Create a simple questionnaire that can be answered by pull-down menus. Limit your questions to four or five. Surveys are the most effective when employees see how the survey modifies corporate behavior. After receiving information from the first 2,000 employees, create a web page that displays the responses.

For example, if the company wanted to make sure an HR benefit site was providing the necessary information, a questionnaire might be displayed after an employee accesses the benefit site.

Sample Questionnaire

1. Did you find the information you were looking for? 1–10
   (1 = all information, 10 = no information)

2. Was the information presented in a way that was easy for you to understand? 1–10 (1 = very easy, 10 = very difficult)
3. Did you have any problem locating the information on this site? 1–10 (1 = easy , 10 = difficult)
4. Do you prefer using on-line access to get information or the company's traditional approach of sending paper to your in-basket? 1–10 (1 = web site, 10 = paper)

Thank employees for being part of the survey. Tell the employees how this information is going to be used. Tell them when the results will be available. Choose the type of information that lends itself easily to being graphed and statistically categorized. Tell the employees what score the department is shooting for. If the goal is met, congratulate the department for creating an effective site. If a question falls below the goal, clearly state this fact. Lay out a clear list of action items the department will perform to increase satisfaction with the site. If the reason for the low mark is obvious, state the reason, the solution, and the time frame for updating the site. Provide an info e-mail so employees can mail in comments or suggestions. If you don't know if you are going to read or respond to all info e-mails, clearly state this up front. A bad mark for a site is not a bad mark for a department. This is new technology. A low score is an area that the department needs to work on in order to create an effective and efficient tool. Treat low marks as opportunities. For example, if the questionnaire falls below a certain percentage of satisfaction, the department can state they will:

1. Conduct a series of employee round tables to identify what specifically employees had problems with
2. Welcome e-mail (specify e-mail address) containing constructive solutions
3. Create a project based on employees' responses to get the site working more effectively

Before planning a survey, discuss the downside to the survey. Make sure you plan for criticism of your site. Schedule time and availability to hold employee round tables, to budget changes, and to work with IS to schedule developers to modify the site. A company that continually checks the effectiveness of web applications will continually increase its knowledge and ability to develop effective applications.

Action items used to create better web sites can be displayed on the department's web page. A project like this can create more than an effective web application. It can foster a sense of team building and group harmony. Employees who feel as if they are being listened to are happier and more productive. When employees' feedback is listened to and responded to, employees are willing to continually provide feedback. The better the communication, the more effective the site, the happier the employees, the more profitable the company.

Making Your Site a Destination Location

By now you should have a good fundamental grasp of what is necessary to create a good web site for your company. It is a good idea to keep your pulse on what companies are doing to keep their web sites current and interesting. A good way to find interesting web sites is to check out "What's Hot" and "What's New" locations on the Internet. Most large Internet centric sites have these locations. For example, if you are using Netscape Navigator, the browser will be preconfigured to have you access Netscape's home page; similarly Microsoft's Internet Explorer is preconfigured to bring up Microsoft's home page. Both of these companies have What's Hot and What's New sections. Most of the web search engines, like Yahoo, Lycos, and Excite, also rank their favorite sites. These companies employ people who spend their day surfing the Internet, exploring new sites and updating their lists. By viewing these pages you can get a lot of insight into what qualities makes a "hot" site. Hot sites are visited sites. If your Internet site's goal is to create company recognition or you are selling a consumer product, you probably want to create a destination location.

Two of my favorite sites are the Jelly Belly and Berkeley Systems sites. I think both companies have created interesting destination locations that spotlight their products.

Figure 8-2. Jelly Belly Home Page

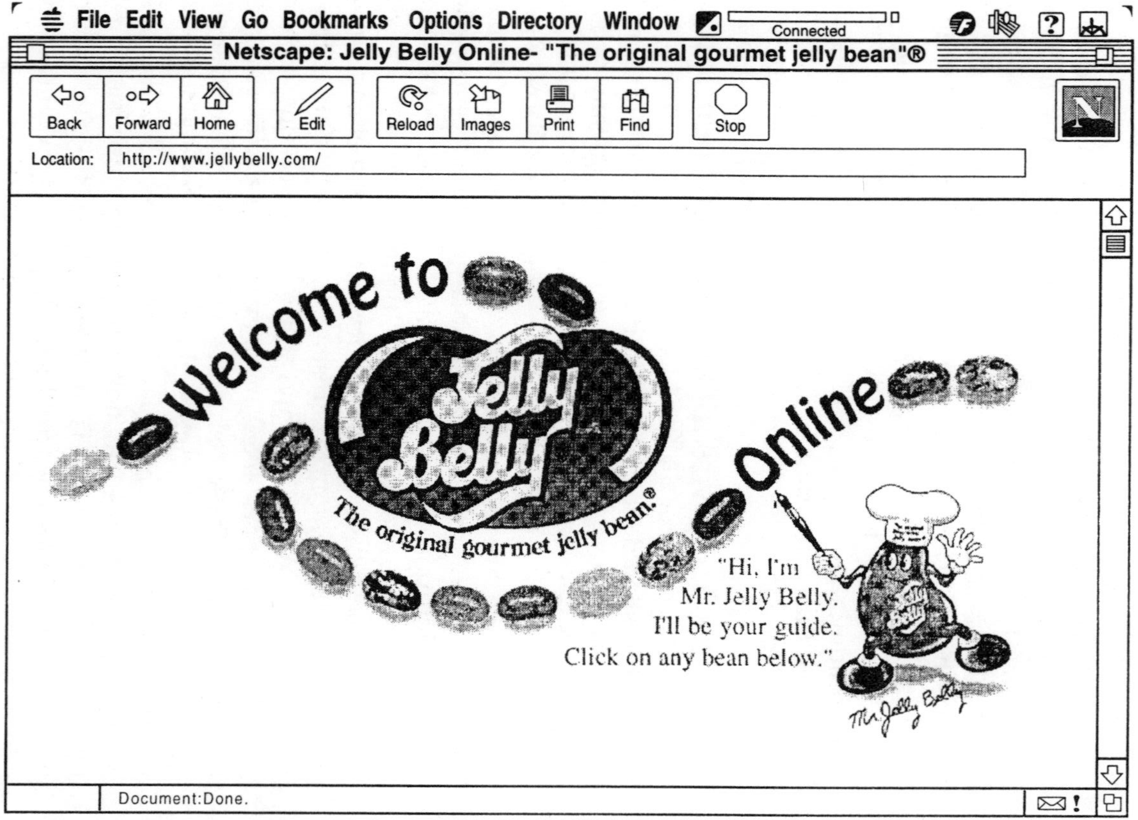

Herman Goelitz Candy is a confectioner in Fairfield, California, famous for its Jelly Belly gourmet jelly beans. Tourists can visit Herman Goelitz and receive a tour of its candy-making facility. While at the facility people can view the company's art gallery of classic paintings remade with Jelly Belly jelly beans, receive a recipe book detailing how to mix Jelly Belly flavors to make a new flavor, or receive a sample of a new Jelly Belly flavor. The companies goal when it created its web site was to introduce its product to a wider audience and create wider brand recognition. Management decided to piggyback their web site to the great success they have had with their Jelly Belly factory tours. Currently Herman Goelitz has over 10,000 visitors a week touring their facility. They wanted a larger, more geographically diverse audience to receive the same personal experience. They decided to set their web site up to be a virtual tour. Visitors to the web site can learn how Jelly Belly jelly beans are created. Virtual visitors can stroll through the Jelly Belly art gallery, where they can view the likes of the *Mona Lisa* portrayed with jelly beans. Jelly Belly flavors and recipes can be viewed in up to fifteen languages. Herman Goelitz decided not to sell their candy products directly through their site because they did not want to compete with their distribution channel. The company decided instead to sell Jelly Belly merchandise from its web site. Loyal Jelly Belly fans can buy Jelly Belly T-shirts, sweatshirts, and baseball caps. To make the experience flavorful, the first 500 visitors who fill out a short questionnaire get mailed a Jelly Belly sampler. The company found demand for the free Jelly Belly jelly beans to be high. At first they fulfilled the first 500 orders each day. They found out this was unfair to West Coast customers. Management decided to open the free site at intermittent hours to provide a level playing field. They have found the site to be easy to manage, since they used an ISP and worked with an art firm to create an interesting location. They feel the site has increased their brand recognition. Herman Goelitz found they did have to beef up their fulfillment organization to support the increase in orders and to fulfill the free shipments.

Berkeley Systems, the creator of Flying Toaster screen savers, has done an excellent job of creating an interesting destination location. The company wanted to create a destination

Figure 8-3. Berkeley Systems Home Page

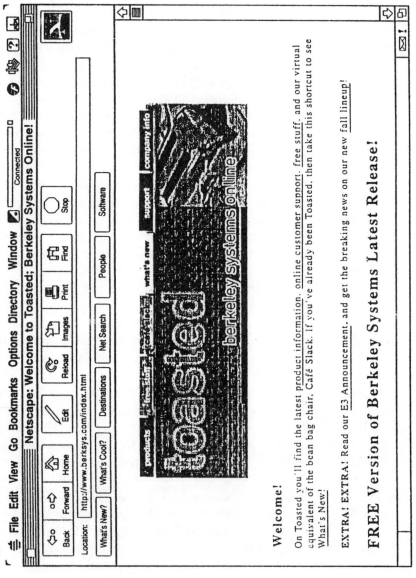

location that would create web traffic so it could spotlight its web products. Berkeley Systems realized people would visit their site for the novelty factor. They figured that while at their site, web surfers would become acquainted with their product line. Their site does contain the on-line brochure, company news, and product-ordering sections found on most companies' web pages. Berkeley Systems has done a good job of not overwhelming the visitor with product and company information by creating banners and short product highlights. Up front and easily accessible from the home page is their free giveaway section and their Cafe Slack. These are the sections they created to provide web traffic. At the time this book is being written, Cafe Slack features Miss Hayne, an irreverent host to the site's interesting contests and events. On one visit to Miss Hayne I got to view the latest Cyber Beauty Pageant contestants, read Miss Hayne's advice column, and see the pictures from Miss Hayne's night on the town. Berkeley Systems has found Miss Hayne to be a popular destination location for cyber surfers.

The Future

Internet technology might be new business technology, but it is easy to see where it is going. The Internet is to the 90s what the fax was to the 80s. In the 80s it seemed that overnight it become impossible to think of doing work with a company that did not have a fax machine. Within a few years it will become difficult to work with a company that does not have e-mail or a web page. Many business cards already contain people's e-mail address, and much business is conducted using e-mail. We have already begun to see consumers make buying decisions based on information they find on the Internet. In a short time you will find that if your company does not have a web site, you will miss potential sales opportunities.

The real growth of Internet technology in the future will be for intranets. The first step companies will experience is the growth of departmental web sites and e-mail. These technologies will increase communication flow within an organization. Over the next few years there will be an increase in applications that take advantage of Internet technology. Most software companies have introduced or are in the process of introducing intranet versions of their product. IS organizations see the advantage of running Internet server applications and using a ubiquitous client. This next-generation client-server solution will allow companies to expand employee services and increase application support with little effect on employees. Employees will access new applications by clicking on a server icon and downloading an applet. Companies will pay software companies for the server application based on the number of clients being supported. Actual client applications will be free or low-cost. Control of maintaining applications will reside in IS, where the expertise is high. Control of running and using applications will be decentralized, at the client's desktop, where the need exists.

Internet technology is not a revolutionary technology. The reason for its quick acceptance and success is that the underlying technology was in place and market acceptance was immediate. You should view the Internet as another tool available to you to help you better manage and market your company. Most of the concepts discussed in this book take already acceptable principles and practices and tailor them for the Internet. Have some fun, get creative, and figure out how this technology can help you create a more effective environment.

Index